A Love Beyond All Telling

A Love Beyond All Telling

Daily Gospel Reflections for the Advent and Christmas Seasons

YEARS A, B, AND C

Albert Haase, OFM

Paulist Press
New York / Mahwah, NJ

Cover image by Twin Design Studio/Shutterstock.com
Cover and book design by Lynn Else

Library of Congress Cataloging-in-Publication Data
Names: Haase, Albert, 1955– author
Title: Love beyond all telling: daily gospel reflections for the Advent and Christmas seasons: years A, B, and C / Albert Haase, OFM.
Description: Paperback. | New York; Mahwah, NJ: Paulist Press, [2026] | Summary: "This is an original work that consists of reflections for Advent and Christmas seasons"—Provided by publisher.
Identifiers: LCCN 2025038440 (print) | LCCN 2025038441 (ebook) | ISBN 9780809157877 paperback | ISBN 9780809189540 ebook
Subjects: LCSH: Advent sermons | Christmas sermons | Bible. Gospels—Sermons | LCGFT: Sermons
Classification: LCC BV4254.5 .H337 2026 (print) | LCC BV4254.5 (ebook)
LC record available at https://lccn.loc.gov/2025038440
LC ebook record available at https://lccn.loc.gov/2025038441

ISBN 978-0-8091-5787-7 (paperback)
ISBN 978-0-8091-8954-0 (ebook)

Published by Paulist Press
997 Macarthur Boulevard
Mahwah, New Jersey 07430
www.paulistpress.com

Printed and bound in the
United States of America

Contents

CONTENTS

Introduction

"The Virgin Mother longed for him with love beyond all telling." This sentence from the second Preface for Advent is used in the celebration of the Eucharist beginning on December 17. Unquestionably, it is my favorite sentence prayed during the season of Advent, and it has provided the inspiration for these reflections.

Advent attends primarily to two important figures in salvation history: Mary and Jesus. Its spirituality centers on the faith and courage of a young woman who opened the doors of her heart to the invitation of God, welcomed the Word into her life, longed for that Word "with love beyond all telling," and then gave birth to the incarnate Word of God, Jesus of Nazareth. Indeed, what Mary longed for with love beyond all telling was, in fact, divine love beyond all telling enfleshed.

As we journey together during the seasons of Advent and Christmas with the daily Gospel of the eucharistic celebration, let us do what Mary has done: offer hospitality in our hearts to the Word, contemplate it amid our daily comings and goings, and long for it with love beyond all telling. Then, come Christmas Day, let us go tell it on the mountain that God's love beyond all telling has taken on flesh in Jesus of Nazareth.

Albert Haase, OFM
Feast of the Annunciation

The Advent Season

FIRST SUNDAY OF ADVENT, YEAR A

Stay Awake! Matthew 24:37–44

Shepherd One, the papal plane, touched down at O'Hare International Airport on October 4, 1979. Due to the cold, drizzly weather conditions, the papal motorcade was ninety minutes behind schedule. Along with more than a thousand religious brothers who waited to pray Evening Prayer with Pope John Paul II, I sat in St. Peter's Church in downtown Chicago. We had been told that the pope was "running a little bit behind schedule." Not knowing how delayed it was, with the others, I would occasionally turn around and anxiously look at the two large steel doors of St. Peter's. I had hoped to see them swing open at any second, the sign that the pontiff had arrived. The atmosphere was electric, and though we had to wait for over an hour and a half, no one seemed to drift off, lose interest, or leave. Suddenly, the doors swung open, and we could see the blue blinking lights of the police cars reflecting off the wet concrete outside and inside the church's vestibule. Everyone instinctively stood up, and the energetic, fifty-nine-year-old pontiff dressed in his white cassock entered the church. We roared with joy and clapped.

Apart from anticipating a meeting with important dignitaries like the pope, the president, a prime minister, a prince, or a princess, it's rare that we focus on each individual moment and live with such eagerness and expectation. Most of us live daily life as sleepwalkers, doing everything by rote and routine. We turn off the alarm, eat breakfast, brush our teeth, shower, go to work, come home, eat dinner, relax, set the alarm, go to sleep—only to repeat the routine again tomorrow.

Today's Gospel is a clarion call to wake up and live every day with expectancy and anticipation. The season of Advent begins with the reminder that as we start preparations for Christmas, we are challenged to stay awake for the second coming of Christ. Much like the papal motorcade running late due to unforeseen events, so too we are not assured an exact time for the second coming. Our challenge, not only in Advent but throughout all the seasons of our lives, is to keep our eyes peeled to the present moment and be vigilant for the unexpected hour when the doors are thrown open and a dignitary no more illustrious than the Prince of Peace himself enters.

PONDER

- How much does waiting for the second coming of Christ impact my life? Why?
- What spiritual practices help me stay awake and be vigilant?

FIRST SUNDAY OF ADVENT, YEAR B

Do What You Are Doing: Mark 13:33–37

I was stopped at a stoplight. I noticed the bumper sticker on the car in front of me. "Jesus is coming soon. Look busy!" I chuckled as I thought to myself, *They got it partially correct.*

If parents leave for a weekend away, their teenagers might be given chores to do and instructions. The parents might tell them, "Don't forget to take out the garbage. Walk the dog after breakfast and in the evening. Cut the grass. Don't leave your dirty dishes in the sink—either wash them by hand or rinse them and put them in the dishwasher."

Our Gospel today likens us to servants who have each been given a task to complete while our master is gone on a trip to a foreign land. We are to not only do what we have been tasked to do but also be attentive to the master's sudden return—because it might catch us off-guard. We don't want to be found nodding off or even worse, asleep. Indeed, we are given a firm order: "Watch!"

By virtue of our baptism, we each have been given a mission to help prepare for the return of the master in the second coming of Christ. The challenge for each of us is to discern that mission as we grow from childhood through adolescence to adulthood. As a spouse, parent, single person, religious, or ordained minister, our mission is made concrete in the occupation we assume over time: preacher, pilot, park ranger, plant manager, pharmacist, painter, professor, pianist, pediatrician, publisher, or psychologist. More than simply looking busy, we must commit wholeheartedly to our mission and stay engaged with it since the second coming of Christ depends on us doing our part. We must not grow weary or be discouraged by the tedium of our tasks.

Before he became the 266th pope of the Roman Catholic Church, Pope Francis was responsible for the young Jesuit scholastics studying for the priesthood. He used to give them wise advice that sums up today's Gospel message: "Do what you are doing but do it well." More than simply looking busy as a bumper sticker suggests, the Gospel challenges us to stay engaged—and awake—as we await the return of our master.

PONDER

- How can I help prepare for the second coming of Christ?
- When do I become weary or discouraged by the tedium of the tasks I am called to complete?

FIRST SUNDAY OF ADVENT, YEAR C

A New Transition: Luke 21:25–28, 34–36

Transitions can be very stressful. I still remember the stress and strain I experienced as I left for the island of Taiwan to begin studies in the Chinese language and culture. I had to get used to new ways of thinking, speaking—and even eating with chopsticks.

Another transition occurred when I moved to mainland China two years later and I was challenged to be careful about revealing my identity as a Franciscan priest.

Twelve years later, I went through still another transition when I was forced to return to the United States after the Security Police of Beijing discovered my identity. I returned to my native country—I thought I was going "home"—only to find myself a stranger among a generation of Franciscans whom I didn't know and who only knew me as "the friar in China." There were television shows and music and even popular slang expressions like Homer Simpson's "D'oh!" meaning "well, that was obvious!" that were unfamiliar to me. There is no doubt that transitions can be surprising, overwhelming, distressing, and disruptive.

Today the Church experiences a transition as we begin a new liturgical year. The Gospel speaks of a specific and final transition—the end of the world! Jesus casts the end in the most frightening of terms with cosmic dismay and people dying of fright as the Son of Man comes on a cloud with power and great glory. In the midst of this cataclysmic event, he challenges us to stand erect with our heads raised because this is the definitive moment we have been awaiting, the final act of redemption. He concludes by encouraging us not to be caught off-guard with life's anxieties or temptations.

The point is obvious: Moments of change and transition, painful, confusing, or seemingly earth-shattering as they can be, are the very moments we are called to put our faith into action and trust in a God whose love is beyond all telling.

PONDER

- When was the last moment of change and transition in my life? How did I initially respond to it?
- When I look back on all the changes and transitions in my life, what have I learned about God's relationship with me?

MONDAY OF THE FIRST WEEK OF ADVENT

Switching Shoes: Matthew 8:5–11

Sensitivity is both a gift and a skill. Some people are born with the facility to put themselves in another's shoes and see the world from that different point of view. This new perspective changes the way they act and relate with other people. But sensitivity is also a skill that we should learn as we mature to adulthood. It affords us the insight to know when to bend the rules or even to ignore some teaching of our upbringing or our culture.

The centurion in today's Gospel is clearly someone of extraordinary sensitivity. According to Roman law, he would have had the right to kill his servant because the law stipulated that any servant who became ill or injured to the point where one could no longer work was no longer worthy of life. Perhaps the centurion sensed the injustice of having one's life defined by an occupation and the sinfulness of considering human life expendable when one's culture labeled it useless. And so, the centurion goes in search of a cure.

In his time of personal need, when most people would be focused on themselves, the centurion, surprisingly, displays a marvelous sensitivity toward Jesus. He wants to spare Jesus the awkward challenge of entering a Gentile home that, according to Jewish custom, would have rendered Jesus unclean. And so, he simply asks Jesus to pronounce the words of healing from afar. Perhaps Jesus's amazement, noted by the evangelist, is partially rooted in the centurion's unexpected sensitivity toward both the paralyzed servant and the divine physician.

Advent is a good time to take an honest look at our own lives and ask if we are growing in the gift and skill of sensitivity. It is a time to confront the injustices and sinfulness that our culture has conditioned us to accept. It is a time to put ourselves in the shoes of others and see the world from different vantage points.

PONDER

- When was the last time that I put myself in the shoes of another and tried to see a situation from a different point of view? What was that like?
- What are some culturally approved injustices and sins? How have my upbringing and education allowed these injustices and sins free reign in my life?

TUESDAY OF THE FIRST WEEK OF ADVENT

A Childlike Quality That Brings Joy: Luke 10:21–24

At the beginning of chapter 10 of Luke's Gospel, Jesus commissions the seventy-two. He sends them forth on mission with specific instructions. They are sent as envoys of peace who carry no money, no extra sandals, and rely on God and the hospitality of the people to whom they are sent. Their major task is to announce the kingdom, and one way of doing that is by curing the sick.

Immediately before today's Gospel, the seventy-two return from their mission. And they are ecstatic with joy. They affirm how demons were submissive to the name of Jesus. Jesus confirms how he saw Satan fall from heaven as the seventy-two ministered and announced the nearness of the kingdom. He further reminds the seventy-two of their power over snakes, scorpions, and the power of the enemy. Indeed, the seventy-two are invincible and their joy should be placed not on their authority over Satan but on the fact that they will attain a heavenly inheritance.

The seventy-two's joy over the success of their mission lit a fire in Jesus's heart as he rejoices in the Holy Spirit. Today's Gospel gives us a rare glimpse into the personal prayer of Jesus as he thanks and praises the Father for a unique quality that the seventy-two possess but the wise and intelligent don't: childlikeness. While the latter might rely on academic study and hypothetical theories, the seventy-two, like infants, radically depend on God and trust that Jesus has equipped them with everything that they need. Consequently, their very lifestyle becomes the first and foremost proclamation of the kingdom, God's love beyond all telling.

Advent is a time for us to once again become like children. Like the seventy-two's, our proclamation of the kingdom will be judged not on our academic knowledge of the faith but on our childlike life of dependence, reliance, and trust in God the Father. By our adherence to living out the challenges of Jesus, we not only give him great joy but also accomplish the gracious will of his heavenly Father.

PONDER

- What are some childlike qualities in my own life?
- In what areas of my life do I need greater dependence and trust in God?

WEDNESDAY OF THE FIRST WEEK OF ADVENT

Feeding the Hungry: Matthew 15:29–37

Born and raised in Spain, Chef José Andrés moved to the United States at the age of twenty-one. He settled in Washington, DC, and started volunteering at DC Central Kitchen. As a chef and restaurateur, he saw how important food is, especially for communities in crisis. After the devastating earthquake in Haiti in 2010, he founded World Central Kitchen, an organization that heads to the frontlines and provides fresh meals in response to humanitarian, climate, and community crises. WCK has provided meals in countries such as Ukraine, Morocco, Puerto Rico, Gaza, and Lebanon. "My mission is simple," Andrés recently told a reporter, "I feed hungry people in crisis."

Jesus could say the same. The first part of today's Gospel reminds us that Jesus satisfied the cravings and longings of people in crisis, specifically the lame, the blind, the deformed, the mute, and people with other ailments. His healings were one of the many ways that he symbolically fed people.

But let's not forget that much of Jesus's ministry was centered around the table and physical food. Indeed, he was a target of criticism precisely because of his table fellowship with sinners. He's even referred to as a "glutton" (see Matthew 11:19).

In the second part of today's Gospel, Jesus is moved with compassion for the people who have followed him up the mountain. They are hungry and Jesus does not want to send them away without first feeding them for fear they might collapse on the way home. With seven loaves and a few fish, he manages to satisfy the physical hunger of the entire crowd—with seven baskets of leftovers!

There is something innately divine in breaking and sharing bread. Indeed, heaven is often depicted as a banquet where all are welcomed and have their hunger satisfied.

During the season of Advent, we reflect on the hungers of the heart and how Jesus became the Bread of Life and was born in an animal feeding trough.

PONDER

- What are the cravings and longings of my heart?
- How does Jesus, the Bread of Life, satisfy my spiritual hunger?

THURSDAY OF THE FIRST WEEK OF ADVENT

Listening and Living: Matthew 7:21, 24–27

Standing at 1,380 feet, the Jin Mao Tower in Shanghai, China, ranks as one of the tallest buildings in the world. To ensure its commercial success and its ability to withstand 125-mph winds, the number 8, an auspicious number in Chinese culture, played a dominant role in its design and dedication. The building has eighty-eight stories, and each vertical segment of the building is one-eighth smaller than the sixteen-story base. The vertical elements also include an octagonal-shaped core surrounded by eight exterior composite columns and eight exterior steel columns. Located at 88 Century Boulevard, the grand opening was held on 8/28/98.

The son of a carpenter, Jesus offers his own blueprint for success and protection against the storms of life in today's Gospel. In doing so he presents the kingdom's way of standing tall. He emphatically states that the ability to perform healings, exorcisms, and miracles in his name—those who say, "Lord, Lord!"—is as likely to get us into the kingdom of heaven as belief in the auspicious number 8 is to guarantee success and protection; rather, Jesus says that success and protection come from building our lives on the foundation of God's will.

And lest we be uncertain about what exactly is the will of God, Jesus states that it consists of two tasks: listening to his words and putting them into action. Listening and living our lives in response to his words about God's unconditional love, God's mercy and compassion, and God's daily protection and providence provide a rock foundation that no storm, tragedy, or trial can shake. Mere listening without building our lives on those words leaves us dangerously vulnerable to the elements, and once the storm sets in, results in our houses collapsing and being completely ruined.

The Scriptures remind us that the Lord is an "eternal Rock" (Isaiah 26:4) and to build our lives on that rock is to stand tall in the kingdom of heaven.

PONDER

- How can I find time in my daily schedule to listen to the words of Jesus and act on them in a practical way?
- Do my words and actions point to a life built on sand or rock? Why?

FRIDAY OF THE FIRST WEEK OF ADVENT

The Gift of Sight: Matthew 9:27–31

In March of 1981, UPI correspondent Jack M. Kneece interviewed Bob Edens. Blind from birth, Edens underwent a complicated surgery that gave him eyesight after fifty-one years.

"I never would have dreamed that yellow was so...so yellow. I don't have the words. I am amazed by yellow. But red is my favorite color. I just can't believe red.

"Grass is something I had to get used to. I always thought it was just fuzz. But to see each individual green stalk, and to see the hair on my arm growing like trees, and birds flying through the air, and everything—it's like starting a whole new life. It's the most amazing thing in the world to see things you never thought you'd see.

"I saw the purple and orange recently in the face of a tiger. I could see the individual hairs and the colors and his eyes.

"I can see the shape of the moon—and I like nothing better than seeing a jet plane flying across the sky leaving a vapor trail. And of course, sunrises and sunsets.

"I can't wait to get up each day to see what I can see. I am still seeing most of it for the first time. And at night I look at the stars in the sky and flashing lights....

"Everything is like a constant high. You could never know how wonderful everything is. I saw some bees the other day, and they were magnificent. And I jumped a covey of quail. I had heard quail before, but to see them flying—Ah...what an experience.

"I saw a truck drive by in the rain the other day and throw a spray into the air. It was marvelous. And did I mention, I saw a falling leaf, just drifting through the air?"

Hearing about Eden's miracle, the late radio commentator

Charles Osgood said, "Once Bob Edens could not see the way we see. Now we cannot see the way Bob Edens sees."

Today's Gospel of the healing of the two blind men gives us cause to pause and ponder the gift of physical sight. Jesus's question to the blind men—and to us—"Do you believe that I can do this?" is a reminder that faith gives us the gift of spiritual sight. Spiritual sight complements physical sight: we are reminded during Advent that we can see God's love beyond all telling in the flesh of a baby born in Bethlehem.

PONDER

- What are some of the most memorable things I have seen in creation?
- How does my spiritual sight help me to see with my physical eyes?

SATURDAY OF THE FIRST WEEK OF ADVENT

Becoming a "Little Christ": Matthew 9:35—10:1, 5a, 6–8

There is so much suffering, sadness, tragedy, and turmoil in the world. The governments of some countries have collapsed and are now controlled by roaming bandits and gangs. Refugees are forced to leave behind their lifestyles and livelihoods and go in search of hospitable countries with strange customs and unintelligible languages. Some people are denied basic human rights and freedoms. Spouses struggle to rebuild trust after an act of infidelity. Children care for elderly parents suffering the confusion and silence of Alzheimer's disease. Parents work two and three jobs to ensure an adequate lifestyle and education for their children.

Suffering and sadness are certainly nothing unique to the twenty-first century. In today's Gospel, upon seeing the crowd "troubled and abandoned, like sheep without a shepherd," Jesus was moved with pity. The Greek word for "pity" has the same root as the word for "bowels," thus suggesting that Jesus's emotion is a deep-seated, heartfelt compassion—the kind that makes a person's heart ache. Perhaps aware that the sadness and desperation were too much for only one to heal, Jesus calls his twelve apostles and gives them the very same authority to cure the sick, raise the dead, cleanse lepers, and drive out demons that the Father had given to him. Clearly, the twelve apostles were sent to do for others what Jesus himself had done.

The name "Christian" literally means "little Christ" and that suggests the baptismal challenge of continuing Jesus's ministry of compassion and the mission entrusted to the twelve apostles. Jesus now sends us out every day—to the kitchen, the classroom, the office, the nursery—to experience the heartache of the world and to embody his compassion by alleviating the suffering, sadness, and desperation that we encounter.

In the words that are often attributed to St. Teresa of Ávila, "Christ has no body now but yours; no hands, no feet on earth but yours; yours are the eyes through which he looks with compassion on this world; Christ has no body now on earth but yours."

PONDER

- Who are the suffering, the sad, and the desperate in my life? In what practical ways can I embody the compassion of Jesus for them?
- In today's news, whose cries for help go unanswered by the world community—and by me?

SECOND SUNDAY OF ADVENT, YEAR A

Prepare the Road to Your Heart: Matthew 3:1–12

I was living in Beijing when the International Olympic Committee (IOC) visited the Chinese capital in 2000 to evaluate its viability and suitability to host the 2008 Summer Olympics. The city had four strong competitors: Paris, Toronto, Osaka, and Istanbul. Three weeks before the IOC arrived, factories on the outskirts of the city were shut down to keep air pollution down to a minimum. A new traffic law went into effect that only allowed automobiles with license plates ending in an odd number to travel into the city on odd numbered days and automobiles with license plates ending in an even number to travel into the city on even numbered days. Two days before the IOC arrived, large stone flowerpots with blossoming trees were situated throughout the city and the streets were cleaned. Never had I seen the city look so dashing and welcoming. On July 13, 2001, the IOC announced that Beijing had beaten its competitors and was awarded the 2008 Olympic games. The city's preparation had paid off.

People in the ancient world also knew the importance of preparing for visiting dignitaries. They would send workers ahead to fill in potholes and to level the bumpy parts of the roads to their destination. This would ensure a safe, smooth, and comfortable trip for the dignitary's carriage or chariot.

Today's Gospel associates Isaiah's prophecy with the ministry of John the Baptist: "A voice of one crying out in the desert, Prepare the way of the Lord, make straight his paths." John is entrusted with the task of preparing the highways and byways to our hearts so that we can receive the one who will baptize with the Holy Spirit and fire. That preparation cannot rely simply on our relationship with the great patriarch Abraham but involves each one of us producing the fruit of good deeds as evidence of our heart's repentance. Only then will we be poised to receive divine love beyond all telling.

PONDER

- How am I preparing the highway to my heart during this Advent season?
- What is a practical way that I can help others prepare for Christmas?

SECOND SUNDAY OF ADVENT, YEAR B

Be a Pre-Evangelizer: Mark 1:1–8

It's not easy to be an opening act or "warm-up act," especially for a famous singer or band. Sometimes the warm-up act does exactly that and the fans get even more excited about the person or band they have come to hear. At other times, fans are frustrated that they must sit and listen to a singer or group that they have not paid to listen to and often aren't even familiar with.

Yet some rock bands became overnight sensations precisely because they were an opening act. In 1963, Roy Orbison embarked on a tour in the United Kingdom with the Beatles as his opening act. Although Orbison was supposed to be the headline singer, before long, Paul, John, George, and Ringo became coheadliners and by the end of the tour, the Beatles would close out the set. The "fab four," a term coined by Tony Barrow, the Beatles' first publicist, went on to become the best-selling music act in the world, far outshining Orbison.

It's quite easy to think of John the Baptist as the opening act or warm-up act for Jesus. But that is inaccurate. He is first and foremost the fulfillment of Isaiah's prophecy: "Behold, I am sending my messenger ahead of you; he will prepare your way. A voice of one crying out in the desert: 'Prepare the way of the Lord, make straight his paths.'" In contemporary parlance, John emerges in the desert as a "pre-evangelizer." As such, his challenge was to help people remove any obstacles that hindered them from hearing the coming message of Jesus. That included having people confess their sins and undergoing John's baptism of repentance.

Unlike the Beatles who would ultimately leapfrog over Orbison and his success, John had no pretensions—he was very much aware of who he was, his personal mission, and where his focus should be. By his own admission, "One mightier than I is coming after me. I am not worthy to stoop and loosen the thongs of his sandals. I have baptized you with water; he will baptize you with the Holy Spirit."

Like John the Baptist, we too are called to be pre-evangelizers. Our baptismal commitment entrusts us with the mission of helping others open their hearts to the transformative good news of God's love beyond all telling enfleshed in the person of Jesus.

PONDER

- What spiritual practices help to keep my heart open to the good news of Jesus?
- How aware am I of the call to be a pre-evangelizer? Among my family and friends, whose heart might need opening to the Gospel message?

SECOND SUNDAY OF ADVENT, YEAR C

God's Unexpected Surprise: Luke 3:1–6

"Once upon a time there was a young boy who dreamed of becoming an NFL field goal kicker. He realized his dream and one day kicked the longest field goal in NFL history."

The first four words—"once upon a time"—alert us to the possibility that this could be a fairy tale, fable, or legend. However, if the narrator had said, "During the presidency of George H. W. Bush, a young boy was born in Houston, Texas. He dreamed of becoming an NFL field goal kicker. In 2021, during the presidency of Joe Biden, he not only realized his dream but kicked the longest field goal in NFL history—sixty-six yards to be exact," we would know know that the narrator was talking about the historic accomplishment of Justin Tucker of the Baltimore Ravens.

In today's Gospel, Luke wants to situate the ministry of John the Baptist in a precise moment of history. Tiberius Caesar was emperor; Pontius Pilate was governor; Herod and his brother, Philip, and Lysanias were tetrarchs; Annas and Caiaphas were the high priests.

But the evangelist is not simply interested in giving us a history lesson. He is also saying something else—something critical of governmental officials and institutional clergymen. Despite the size of the empire, the Word of God did not come to Tiberius Caesar. Nor did it come to the powerful governor or Herod, his brother, or Lysanias. And surprisingly, Annas and Caiaphas, the institutional clergymen who alone could enter the Holy of Holies, were also passed by.

To prepare the way and proclaim his coming love beyond all telling, God chose a man who had no power and was not known for his piety. Surprisingly, it was a man on the periphery: "John the son of Zechariah," a very common name at the time, who lived "in the desert," a place where most people ventured into only by necessity. Such a divine choice speaks volumes about the marginalized and those on the sidelines standing center stage in salvation history. They become God's mouthpiece.

During Advent, we remind ourselves that God uses the most unexpected people in the most ordinary of circumstances to prepare and proclaim a love beyond all telling.

PONDER

- What unexpected people and events has God used to express a lavish love for me?
- When have I been called to challenge political or religious institutions?

MONDAY OF THE SECOND WEEK OF ADVENT

Climbing the Roof: Luke 5:17–26

"My uncle is in the hospital and in critical condition, Father. Since his divorce some twenty years ago, he hasn't been to church. He always says he's no longer worthy. Would you mind going to visit him? I honestly think he wants to get back to church, but he just doesn't know how."

I went to visit the man. Over the course of our two-hour visit, I clarified some of his misconceptions, heard his confession, and celebrated the sacrament of the anointing of the sick with him. As I left the hospital, I was grateful for his niece who was aware of how her uncle was paralyzed by his situation and who went out of her way to make him aware of God's love beyond all telling.

In today's Gospel, we encounter a man who is also paralyzed by his sins. Indeed, in Jesus's day, people believed that physical sickness was a result of one's personal sins or those in one's family. We don't know whether the paralytic requested Jesus's help—all we know is that some men, unable to carry this paralytic to Jesus because of the crowd, went out of their way to climb the roof, open a hole, and lower their friend right in front of Jesus. The Gospel states emphatically that it was "their faith" that moved Jesus to forgive the paralytic and ultimately heal him.

The point is obvious: There are so many people in our lives who are paralyzed by their sins and alienated from the Church. Behind rationalizations, anger, and confusion are women and men who are sometimes anxious to experience the mercy and love of God. But life being as it is, they don't always know how to get there.

That's where we come in. Our faith challenges us, contemporary friends of the paralytic, to find appropriate ways to bring that uncle, that child, that spouse to Jesus. When we encounter obstacles, we need to think about creative ways to climb the roof.

PONDER

- Who has helped me come back to Jesus?
- Who in my life needs to be "lowered down through the roof" to Jesus? What are some practical ways that I can do that?

TUESDAY OF THE SECOND WEEK OF ADVENT

An Incomplete Flock: Matthew 18:12–14

Brenda was heartbroken. Her oldest son was sentenced to three years in prison. "I'm having a hard time dealing with this situation," she told me on Christmas Eve. "The holidays are about family and mine is broken. It's incomplete without Sam sitting at the Christmas table with us."

Today's short Gospel packs more punch than most people notice. The fact that the shepherd has a flock of one hundred sheep clearly suggests a man of means—or someone who has lived up to the first-century reputation that shepherds didn't hesitate to steal others' sheep. Because of this reputation, they often were lumped together with tax collectors and prostitutes as people who could not be saved.

One hundred was considered a whole number so having only ninety-nine implies the flock is not complete and whole; hence the shepherd's decision to search for the sheep who has gone astray. The fact that we are not told if he counted his sheep or just knew by sight that one was missing shows a keen sensitivity and investment in each sheep.

We are told that "if" the shepherd manages to find his errant sheep—it's clearly not a done deal—he will rejoice more over the find than over the ninety-nine that did not go astray. Then comes the moral of the story: "In just the same way, it is not the will of your heavenly Father that one of these little ones be lost."

The parable suggests, as Brenda instinctively knew, that every single sheep is important for the wholeness and unity of the flock. When someone strays from the flock for whatever reason, the person's absence affects the entire community. We are lacking the person's presence, gifts, and talents that help us be who we are called to be.

Although we often interpret Jesus as the searching shepherd, the parable's moral suggests that those who do the will of the Father have the responsibility of searching out those who have gone astray and returning them to the fold so the community can be made whole.

PONDER

- Among my family and friends, whom do I consider an errant sheep? How can I bring that person back to the love, care, and concern of the community?
- When have I gone astray? Who helped to bring me back into the community?

WEDNESDAY OF THE SECOND WEEK OF ADVENT

The "Yoke of the Law": Matthew 11:28–30

At the time of Jesus, a well-made yoke was important if a farmer wanted to harness the maximum strength of two healthy oxen. Such a yoke would distribute the load evenly between the two beasts of burden, thus making the work easier on each. It would also follow the contours of the oxen's necks so it would not rub or chafe. There is an old legend that says in his carpenter's shop, Jesus made the best ox-yokes in all Galilee.

Although this is the imagery behind today's beloved Gospel passage, Jesus is really saying something much more important than simply making a sales pitch for his yokes. He is talking about the Jewish Law and one's relationship to it.

God had given the Law to Moses on Mount Sinai to call the chosen people to justice, mercy, and faithfulness. Over the years, the Pharisees began to refer to it as the "yoke of the Law" and believed that through strict obedience to it, they could offer God their maximum spiritual strength and worship. With the best of intentions, they began to add to it and embellish it. Submission to these man-made additions to the "yoke of the Law" made it a heavy burden that weighed down even the most pious of Jews and rubbed against and chafed the human heart. More tragically, the whole purpose of God's gift of the Law was lost.

Jesus understood a pharisaical mentality could skew religious devotion. In today's Gospel, he invites us to unburden ourselves of blind obedience and join him in the harness of his yoke. His yoke is easy because he promises to take the lead. Following his example of meekness and humility, we will find ourselves going beyond a legalistic approach to God's Law and working the field of justice, mercy, and faithfulness God originally intended. It is there where we offer God our spiritual worship and find refreshment for the tasks ahead.

PONDER

- When am I tempted to emphasize strict obedience to God's Law over and above the Law's purpose of justice, mercy, and faithfulness?
- How do I know if I really have joined Jesus in the harness of his yoke? When have I been tempted to take the lead away from him?

THURSDAY OF THE SECOND WEEK OF ADVENT

Identifying Decisive Events: Matthew 11:11–15

Some events in history are so definitive and decisive that everything changes after they occur. Sometimes they happen almost imperceptibly, such as when Ray Tomlinson created the first email program in 1971. Others are witnessed around the world via television, such as Neil Armstrong walking on the moon on July 20, 1969, the fall of the Berlin Wall on November 9, 1989, or the terrorist attacks against the United States on September 11, 2001. In such cases, people wake up the following day to a very different world.

At the time of Jesus, hopes and expectations of a coming messiah had been swirling around the rocky paths and dusty marketplaces of Palestine for a long time. For some, these hopes centered on a political messiah who would overcome the Romans and drive them out of the promised land. For others, these expectations had a cosmic air, suggesting that the Messiah would be preceded by the arrival of the prophet Elijah—identified by Jesus in today's Gospel as John the Baptist—who would help inaugurate the decisive new age of God's kingdom (see Sirach 48:10; Malachi 3:23).

In today's Gospel, Matthew the evangelist is stating that a definitive and decisive event has occurred in history with the life and ministry of Jesus. Although imperceptible to some and violently opposed by others, the arrival of Jesus on the scene now makes the world a very different place than what it previously had been. Jesus associates the kingdom of heaven with God's unconditional care and concern for the poor, the outcasts, and those on the margins of society. Before political and cosmic expectations, Jesus as Messiah is first and foremost the incarnation of God's love beyond all telling.

There are definitive events in the personal life of each one of us. We wake up and find the world very different as we assume the role of a committed Christian, spouse, parent, professed religious, or ordained clergy. Hopefully, over time we grow in the awareness that such events call us to the mission of witnessing to the reality of God's kingdom and divine love beyond all telling.

PONDER

- What have been the decisive events in my own personal life? How has my world changed because of them?
- How do I see my personal, decisive events reflecting God's love beyond all telling for me and those around me? What specific mission do they call me to accept?

FRIDAY OF THE SECOND WEEK OF ADVENT

Responding Wholeheartedly: Matthew 11:16–19

Every parent has heard a child make the complaint against a neighbor or sibling, "Billy won't play with me!" Billy's reasons could be countless. Perhaps he fancies himself "too old" for cops and robbers. Perhaps he has other people or activities that momentarily have captured his attention. Perhaps he just is not interested. In any event, the fact remains: Billy doesn't want to respond and play.

Today, Jesus compares his generation of listeners to children in the marketplace desperate for playmates. He likens them to children who pretend to be the pipe players at weddings, but no one dances to their music. He likens them also to children playacting as mourners, sulking when no one joins in their wailing. These two comparisons, innocent as they sound, are ambiguous enough to be open to different interpretations. Each interpretation, however, offers a scathing criticism of Jesus's own contemporary scene.

Perhaps the children represent the scribes and Pharisees with their Law-oriented approach to Judaism. In this case, the religious leaders are portrayed precisely as childish actors who do not arouse the interest or elicit a hearty response from their listeners. Being actors, they have lost touch with reality.

Perhaps the children represent the religious leaders and the listeners who expect John and Jesus to offer God's message on the leaders' and listeners' own terms, in response to their own expectations of how God should be. Thinking they have it figured out correctly, they miss the boat because of their narrow-mindedness and misunderstanding of God's love beyond all telling. John is criticized for being a demon-possessed ascetic and Jesus for being a gluttonous drunk who keeps bad company.

Or perhaps the comparison is simply meant to highlight a more basic reality: the leaders and listeners have hardened their hearts, found other distractions, and consciously refuse to respond to God's message.

Today's Gospel suggests that God's love cannot be refused, boxed in, or accepted on one's own terms. Indeed, it commands a wholehearted response that arises from a heart full of gratitude for a love beyond all telling.

PONDER

- How do I know if my response to God's love is merely childish playacting or the mature expression of a grateful heart?
- When was the last time distractions kept me from deliberately responding to God's love beyond all telling?

SATURDAY OF THE SECOND WEEK OF ADVENT

Reconciling Rifts: Matthew 17:9a, 10–13

Martha always had a hard time getting through the holidays. She would hear her friends talk about getting together with family. Just hearing their joy would exacerbate the pain she felt. She had been alienated from her parents for half a decade and hadn't communicated with her brother and sister for even longer. The older she got, the more she longed to be connected again to her family. She just didn't know how to reconnect.

Martha's good friend Rachel was aware of her friend's longing. And so, a few weeks before Christmas, Rachel decided to host a holiday party. She invited many of her coworkers, among whom was Martha's sister-in-law who brought along her husband, Bill. Rachel also invited Martha.

Martha's heart skipped a beat when she saw her brother, Bill, sitting on the couch. Bill was delighted to see Martha again and instantly stood up and embraced her. They chatted briefly. After getting a plate of snacks, they chatted some more—and then some more. The lines of communication became floods of news and stories in each of their recent pasts.

Right before leaving the party, Martha pulled Rachel aside. "Thank you," she said, "You gave me part of my family back and that's a gift I intend to never lose again."

In today's Gospel, Jesus specifies that John the Baptist is Elijah. In Jewish tradition, Elijah was expected to return before the final day of the Lord to end wrath and to reconcile family members (see Sirach 48:10 from the first reading). Part of John's ministry was to bring about a conversion of hearts so that families could dwell in peace again.

Advent challenges us to look around and see if there are family members with whom we need to be reconciled. It also challenges us to see if we know appropriate ways to help others be reconciled. Indeed, adequate preparation for the Prince of Peace includes our hearts being at peace with our own families. It is often among parents and siblings that we first hear the story of God's love beyond all telling.

PONDER

- Who are the members of my immediate family or extended family with whom I need to be reconciled? How can I be reconciled?
- What can I do to continue the ministry of the prophet Elijah and bring about the healing gift of reconciliation between those who are alienated from one another?

THIRD SUNDAY OF ADVENT, YEAR A

Contains Much, Reveals Little: Matthew 11:2–11

When people ask me, "Are you a priest?" I immediately reply, "Yes." My reply does not indicate if I am a Catholic or Anglican priest, much less a Franciscan priest. And my reply does not indicate how I have ministered as a priest over the years: a preacher, a teacher of both college and graduate students, an author of more than fifteen books, a missionary to mainland China, a spiritual director and trainer of spiritual directors, and the director of Human Resources for a large international accounting firm. That one word "yes" contains so much but reveals so little.

While in prison, John the Baptist heard about the works of the Christ. He sent his disciples to Jesus to ask, "Are you the one who is to come, or should we look for another?" In effect, he was asking Jesus if he was the promised Messiah. For some people, that word "Messiah" contained strong political overtones.

Jesus did not respond with a resounding "Yes!" That one word would not reveal the kind of Messiah he was—one who conveyed God's love beyond all telling. Instead, Jesus replied with the miracles and marvels of his ministry: "The blind regain their sight, the lame walk, lepers are cleansed, the deaf hear, the dead are raised, and the poor have the good news proclaimed to them. And blessed is the one who takes no offense at me."

Jesus's response echoes the words of the first reading from the prophet Isaiah when the prophet proclaims the arrival of our vindicating God who comes to save us. "Then will the eyes of the blind be opened, the ears of the deaf be cleared; then will the lame leap like a stag, then the tongue of the mute will sing." John would have heard in Jesus's reply this ancient prophecy and thus knew the answer to his question was "Yes," but that Jesus would not be a political messiah.

Occasionally, we are asked if we believe in God or are religious. We might be quick to respond with a resounding "Yes!" Better for us to follow Jesus's lead and let our thoughts and actions speak for themselves; they will bolster or betray our response.

PONDER

- How do my thoughts and actions convey my belief in God's love beyond all telling?
- When have my actions helped others come to a deeper belief in God's love beyond all telling?

THIRD SUNDAY OF ADVENT, YEAR B

True Humility: John 1:6–8, 19–28

There is a misconception that true humility is living with one's head held low, eyes fixed to the ground, while fostering the feeling of absolute worthlessness. It sometimes devolves into self-contempt and turns a person into a "doormat for Jesus" where others wipe their feet. It sacrifices all self-respect and self-esteem.

In his book *Thoughts in Solitude*, Thomas Merton famously reminded his readers that "humility is a virtue, not a neurosis." Coming from the Latin word *humus*, which means "dirt" or "ground," it's the wonderful virtue that keeps my feet on the ground and prevents me from being puffed up with pride. It is the fruit of self-knowledge that acknowledges the God with a love beyond all telling has blessed me with gifts and talents and a mission. Humility is also living as a child with absolute dependence on God. As St. Francis of Assisi liked to say, "What you are before God, that you are, and nothing more."

Today's Gospel presents John the Baptist as a man of true humility. The evangelist makes clear that the Baptist was not the light but came "to testify to the light, so that all might believe through him." When asked about his identity, John explicitly stated, "I am not the Christ." He also denied being Elijah or the Prophet. Clearly identifying himself as the precursor of the Messiah, he stated, quoting Isaiah, "I am the voice of one crying out in the desert, make straight the way of the Lord." His mission was to prepare his listeners for the one coming after him whose sandal strap he was not worthy to untie. John knew exactly who he was and what he was called to do as he stood before God.

Advent is a time to rediscover the virtue of humility. John the Baptist offers us one way of rediscovery by honestly pondering the question, "Who am I before God?" The Word of God himself gives us another way by pondering his incarnation as the lowly Babe of Bethlehem.

PONDER

- Who am I before God?
- How does the virtue of humility shape my praise, thanksgiving, and gratitude to God?

THIRD SUNDAY OF ADVENT, YEAR C

Extraordinarily Ordinary: Luke 3:10–18

When you hear the word *saint*, what do you think of? How would you describe a holy person? Do you think of a person who crosses the Atlantic or Pacific Ocean and dedicates years to the foreign missions in Africa or Asia? Is your idea of a holy person someone who spends long hours in daily prayer and penance behind the walls of a monastery? Or do you think of saints as people in service to the poor and disadvantaged of society? Does your idea of sanctity require working for peace, justice, and the integrity of all creation?

Today's Gospel reveals a surprising understanding of holiness. Holiness and sanctity are nothing extraordinary. Perhaps a better way of saying it is that they are extraordinarily ordinary. When the crowds asked how they should respond to his message of repentance, John the Baptist said they should share their clothing and food with those who are less fortunate. In response to the tax collectors, John challenged them to stop overcharging people for taxes. When the soldiers wanted to know how they could live a life in accordance with God's message, the Baptist encouraged a life of fairness, justice, and moderation.

The point is obvious: holiness is not necessarily about grand missionary adventures, taking religious vows, or radically changing one's lifestyle. Many holy people and saints were never presented with such opportunities or choices. Indeed, John's perspective is much more practical: to be a saint means planting our feet firmly in the here and now and bringing the good news to this minute, to this situation. Sanctity is about doing what we already do—but doing it from the awareness of a love beyond all telling.

The readings for this Gaudete Sunday cause us to "shout for joy" and "rejoice in the Lord" because we are all on the way to holiness—if we do what we do with love, peace, and justice.

PONDER

- What occupations and attitudes do I think are challenges for a saint? Which ones are required for a saint?
- What are the areas in my life where I need to grow in holiness?

MONDAY OF THE THIRD WEEK OF ADVENT

A Close Relationship: Matthew 21:23–27

How often have we felt frustrated, surprised, shocked, and stood in disbelief of someone's superior actions or entitled attitude? When we notice someone acting or speaking in an overly confident, demanding, dismissive, arrogant or presumptuous manner, we don't hesitate to say, "Who does he think he is?" "How dare she say that!"

In today's Gospel, though we are not told the words of Jesus, the chief priests and elders of the people are shocked, maybe even scandalized, by Jesus's teachings in the temple area. Jesus's words in the sacred area of the temple elicit from the disturbed leaders two disbelieving questions, "By what authority are you doing these things? And who gave you this authority?" Indeed, it was the first-century's version of "Who do you think you are?"

This confrontational Gospel seems better suited for the season of Lent than Advent. But Jesus's tricky reply, asking the origin of John's baptism—"Was it heavenly or of human origin?"—subtly reminds us that John the Baptist and Jesus had a close ministerial connection. Advent is a time when the relationship between John and Jesus looms large in the Gospel readings.

Unlike Luke, who tells us that John and Jesus were related because John's mother, Elizabeth, was related to Mary (1:36), Matthew does not mention any blood ties. The first Gospel, however, does indicate the close ministerial relationship between the two. John announces that his baptism of repentance with water will be replaced by a baptism with the Holy Spirit and fire by someone who will come after him (3:11–12). Despite his own objection, he baptizes Jesus (3:13–17). John's arrest seems to be the impetus for Jesus to begin his ministry (4:12–17). While in prison, John will send some of his disciples to ask Jesus if he was the Messiah (11:2–6) and upon their return to John, Jesus will openly declare his close ministerial connection to John by naming the Baptist as Elijah, the messenger promised by Isaiah who would prepare the way for the Messiah (11:7–19).

Today's Gospel reminds us that the incarnation of God's love beyond all telling had a rich history that started with Old Testament prophecies, continued with Mary's "yes," was prepared by John the Baptist, and culminated in the ministry of Jesus.

PONDER

- How would I answer an unbeliever who asks me, "Who gave Jesus the authority to say and do the things he said and did?" How much integrity would my answer have?
- How aware am I of the importance of John the Baptist in the history of salvation? Who are the contemporary John the Baptists who help prepare us for the second coming of Christ?

TUESDAY OF THE THIRD WEEK OF ADVENT

Actions Speak Louder Than Words: Matthew 21:28–32

I used to live with a friar who was one of the least dependable people I have ever known. "I'll happily load the dishwasher tonight," he would say after we prayed grace before supper. By the time dessert was served, he would have disappeared. "I'll take the garbage can out" was his mantra that was rarely, if ever, fulfilled. When challenged for his inaction, he would always say, "I said I would do it," as if to suggest that the person who did the chore was overhasty, jumped the gun, and acted too soon.

Today's parable of the two sons is unique to Matthew. A father asks his first son to go work in his vineyard. The son brusquely refuses but afterward, has a change of heart and goes. The father has the same request for the second son. This son responds politely, "Yes, sir." He, however, did not go.

Jesus then asked the chief priests and the elders of the people, "Which of the two did his father's will?" It's not a surprise that they responded with the obvious answer, "The first."

What is a surprise, however, is that Jesus turns the parable into an allegory and, rarely done in the four Gospels, interprets it himself. His interpretation highlights the answer of the chief priest and elders as a self-condemnation. Tax collectors and prostitutes are likened to the first son whose disobedient response was nullified by the appropriate, changed behavior. The chief priests and elders are likened to the second son whose obedient response did not match the appropriate, subsequent action. The religious authorities, presuming to do the will of God, did not change their minds and believe in the message of John the Baptist while the presumed sinners did and are now entering the kingdom. Seeing tax collectors and prostitutes entering the kingdom still did not change the minds of the chief priests and the elders.

Today's Gospel is a reminder that actions speak louder than words. Ideally, our words should align with our actions, but when they don't, it is our actions that betray the depths of our spiritual maturity and our allegiance to the Father's will.

PONDER

- What are the typical, common situations when my actions fail to match my words?
- Whom do I consider to be presumed sinners? How do I react or respond to their sense of having a spiritual life?

WEDNESDAY OF THE THIRD WEEK OF ADVENT

Fulfillment: Luke 7:18b–23

In today's Gospel, Jesus's reply to John's two disciples concerning his identity is a verbatim repetition of what is found in Matthew's Gospel for the Third Sunday of Advent, Year A. Jesus's reply indicates a deep resonance to the Old Testament, especially end-time texts from the prophet Isaiah, that John and his disciples would have instantly recognized.

In the twenty-ninth chapter of the prophet Isaiah, the people of Israel are characterized as refusing to believe in the divine revelation that they will be saved. Toward the end of this chapter, hope for the future is proclaimed and the prophet states, "On that day the deaf shall hear the words of the scroll, and out of their gloom and darkness the eyes of the blind shall see" (29:18).

Perhaps written during the Babylonian exile, chapter 35 of the prophet Isaiah not only speaks of Israel's return from exile but also sings of the transformation of God's people: "Then the eyes of the blind shall be opened, and the ears of the death unstopped; then the lame shall leap like a deer, and the tongue of the speechless sing for joy" (35:5–6). Eyes, ears, limbs, and tongue are all addressed individually and stand for the whole community.

Toward the end of Isaiah's prophecy, we hear the good news of deliverance that Jesus will cite and apply to himself in the synagogue of Nazareth: "The spirit of the Lord God is upon me, because the Lord has anointed me; he has sent me to bring good news to the oppressed, to bind up the brokenhearted, to proclaim liberty to captives, and release to prisoners" (61:1).

Jesus's ministry of healing was the fulfillment of the promise found in the prophet Isaiah. By the explicit citation of his specific miracles, Jesus is not only suggesting his connection to the prophecy of Isaiah but also announcing the definitive fulfillment of God's love beyond all telling.

PONDER

- How have Jesus's teachings and ministry helped me to see and hear the deepest meaning of my life?
- Which teachings of Jesus have been exceptionally good news for me personally?

THURSDAY OF THE THIRD WEEK OF ADVENT

The Measure of Greatness: Luke 7:24–30

An AI search of the question "What makes a person great?" notes different qualities that people have described. They include kindness, compassion, responsibility, honesty, respect, humility, resilience, empathy, integrity, openness, intuition, loyalty, generosity, gratitude, forgiveness, self-forgetfulness, and courage. Each characteristic on its own speaks volumes about how such a person can stand out from the crowd.

Although we often read of John the Baptist preaching who he is as the precursor to Jesus, in today's Gospel we find Jesus noting who John is. He asks the crowd three rhetorical questions, the first two having the obvious answer of "no." John is not a reed swayed by the wind nor some royalty dressed luxuriously and living in a palace. Jesus affirms the answer to his third question, namely, that John is a prophet—and then calls him "more than a prophet." Jesus quotes the first verse from the third chapter of Malachi, the prophet whose death ushered in four centuries of prophetic silence. The Baptist himself, preaching and baptizing in the desert, would break that silence and be the messenger preparing the path for Jesus.

Perhaps it is because John is "more than a prophet" that Jesus declares, "I tell you, among those born of women, no one is greater than John." Then Jesus makes an important statement about greatness: "Yet the least in the kingdom of God is greater than he."

Who are these least in the kingdom of God? Luke offers his own interpretation in his parenthetical comment. They are the people, including tax collectors, who changed their lives, were baptized by John, and acknowledged the righteousness of God that was incarnated in the person of Jesus. In a harsh criticism, Luke states explicitly that the Pharisees and scholars of the Law, who did not accept John's baptism, had rejected the plan of God for themselves.

Today's Gospel challenges us to reflect on our lives and discern if, by God's grace, we have achieved true greatness in the kingdom of God. It consists in having the humility to confess our sins and like a child, accept the free offer of God's love beyond all telling made incarnate in the person of Jesus.

PONDER

- Whom do I consider great among my family and friends? Why?
- What attitudes and actions of mine need to change so that I can accept the invitation into the kingdom of God?

FRIDAY OF THE THIRD WEEK OF ADVENT

Character Witnesses: John 5:33–36

It's not uncommon during the sentencing phase of a trial for the defense to present character witnesses who attest to the defendant's character, reputation, or behavior. They might include family members, friends, neighbors, and even clergy. Having some acquaintance or direct contact with the defendant, character witnesses can offer insights into the defendant's personality, disposition, and temperament that might influence the judge or jury.

Today's Gospel comes from the fifth chapter of the Gospel of John. The passage needs to be put into context for a deeper appreciation of it. The chapter begins with Jesus attending a festival in Jerusalem. Jesus is at a healing pool by the Sheep Gate where the blind, lame, and paralyzed gather in hopes of being cured. Jesus encounters a crippled man who has been ill for thirty-eight years. Learning that the man wants to be healed, Jesus cures him. The man picks up his mat and walks. It is the Sabbath.

When the Jews discovered that it was Jesus who performed the miracle, they began persecuting Jesus "because he was doing such things on the sabbath" (5:16). Today's Gospel is Jesus's defense against the charge of violating the Sabbath. According to the Old Testament (Numbers 35:30 and Deuteronomy 17:6), at least two witnesses were required for testimony in capital cases.

Jesus points to John the Baptist as one of his character witnesses. He calls the Baptist a "burning and shining light" that testified to the truth of Jesus's identity. Unfortunately, the Jews focused on John and not the person his truth was illuminating. Jesus notes that he has testimony greater than John's.

Jesus points to his works as the second witness. They themselves testify on Jesus's behalf that he was sent by the Father.

Today's Gospel not only reminds us again that Advent is a time to reflect on the relationship between John and Jesus but also to ponder the glow of God's love beyond all telling.

PONDER

- What would my family and friends say about my character, reputation, and temperament?
- What do my words and actions say about my character and temperament?

FOURTH SUNDAY OF ADVENT, YEAR A

No Talk, All Action: Matthew 1:18–24

Brother Jerome spent fifty-one of his fifty-four years as a Franciscan friar in San Antonio. He seemed to know everyone, so I wasn't surprised that his funeral at Mission San Jose Church was standing room only. In his homily, a Franciscan priest paid the deceased one of the highest compliments I've ever heard. "Those of us who knew and loved Brother Jerome, knew him as a man of few words. He had the uncanny ability to know what God wanted him to do, and he did it without complaint or fanfare." The spontaneous applause that followed those words confirmed the veracity of that compliment.

We know that Christmas is fast approaching because today's Gospel begins, "This is how the birth of Jesus Christ came about." We might be caught off-guard to see the central figure in today's Gospel is not the Virgin Mary but Joseph, a man who never utters a single word in the Gospels.

The Gospel states explicitly that Joseph had decided to divorce his pregnant fiancée, Mary. It was a done deal—until an angel appeared to him in a dream and offered an explanation steeped in the mystery of God's plan for salvation. Without word or hesitation, when he awoke, Joseph "did as the angel of the Lord had commanded him and took his wife into his home."

Like Brother Jerome, Joseph emerges as an obedient man who discerned God's will and obeyed it without question or doubt. While many people would demand logical explanations when they find themselves in such a precarious situation, Joseph silently bows before the mystery he finds himself engulfed in and obeys. His obedience proclaims the depths of his faith.

Like Brother Jerome and St. Joseph, we are challenged to have an awakened, discerning heart that is open to the mystery of God's love beyond all telling. Indeed, that is an important step for our Advent pilgrimage.

PONDER

- What do I need to know before taking a step in faith? Why?
- How does St. Joseph's example challenge my need for logical and reasonable explanations?

FOURTH SUNDAY OF ADVENT, YEAR B

A Generous Yes: Luke 1:26–38

After receiving his degree in theology, my friend Phil and his wife felt called to be foreign missionaries. They found an organization that was looking for volunteers to help run an orphanage in Malawi. Enquiring about living conditions, Phil discovered that the village he and his wife would live in did not have internet access. He would have to drive three hours for access. "I'm embarrassed to admit it, but that was almost a deal breaker. I'm an avid fantasy football player and I just couldn't see myself abandoning that hobby." After discussing the pros and cons for five months, Phil and his wife found themselves running that orphanage.

To come to a deeper appreciation of today's Gospel of Mary's Annunciation, it's important to know something about the role of women in first-century Palestine. Women could own no property. As a matter of fact, they were considered property. They were the property of their parents and once married off, they became the property of their husbands. And so, the only thing a woman could conceivably call her own was her reputation. And it was precisely her reputation that God asked Mary to sacrifice in requesting her to be the mother of the Son of God.

With a generosity beyond all telling, Mary's response is stunning and astonishing: "Behold, I am the handmaid of the Lord. May it be done to me according to your word."

As Phil's and Mary's experiences make obvious, the call of God is sometimes disconcerting, daunting, and demanding. It challenges us to ponder our lives and discover our deepest desires and priorities. It demands that we live with our hands wide open, never clinging to something as superficial as fantasy football or as deep-seated as one's reputation. God's call is always a call to freedom.

As Christmas approaches, we are reminded of the sacrifices of a virgin and of the Son of God who took on human flesh.

PONDER

- When have I hesitated to respond to the call of God because I chose to cling to some personal desire or longing? Why?
- How does Mary's generosity challenge me?

FOURTH SUNDAY OF ADVENT, YEAR C

Divine Encounters: Luke 1:39–45

Christmas is right around the corner and many of us will already be excited as we begin making last-minute planning and preparations for the Christmas feast. Some of us might do last-minute buying and wrapping gifts. Most of us will prepare for visits from family and friends, some of whom we normally do not see. It's not yet Christmas, but the air might very well be electric with our anticipation and preparation for its arrival.

Today's Gospel of the Visitation is filled with the same electricity of anticipation and preparation as two pregnant women meet. Elizabeth is beyond childbearing years and yet miraculously ready to soon give birth as the baby joyfully kicks in her womb. Mary is young, radiant with stunning faith, bearing a son and longing for him with love beyond all telling. Although the traditional custom of the day would oblige the younger to greet the elder, it is Elizabeth who recognizes the sanctity of such a visit, as the mother of the Lord unexpectedly comes into her home and life. She greets Mary with a salutation that sings of her dignity and role in salvation history: "Most blessed are you among women, and blessed is the fruit of your womb." Busy and caught up in her own private joy, Elizabeth pauses to acknowledge the presence of the other.

The Visitation reveals to us the sacredness of every visit by a relative, friend, neighbor, or foe. Whether planned or unexpected, short or lengthy, each is a divine encounter. Every person is worthy, consecrated, and sent forth with a God-given dignity and mission: like Mary, to be a living tabernacle of love beyond all telling.

As the Feast of Christmas approaches, the doorbell will ring often. As we open the door and greet a familiar or unfamiliar face, let's not forget that our words and deeds can convey the same excitement and recognition that Elizabeth had in welcoming Mary into her home: "Blessed are you."

PONDER

- Who are the people I often encounter in my life, and how are they the blessed of God?
- How can I better approach others as a tabernacle of God's love beyond all telling?

DECEMBER 17

The Good, the Bad, and the Ugly: Matthew 1:1–17

Finding Your Roots with Henry Louis Gates, Jr. is a popular television program on PBS. In each episode, Gates, a renowned Harvard scholar and historian, shares genealogical information with celebrities. People as diverse as musician Dionne Warwick, comedian Tracy Morgan, and actor Michael Douglas have received information about their family roots, secrets about their lineage, and sometimes unexpected relationships with famous people, all researched by professional genealogists. The show's popularity is partially based on the continuing interest with DNA tests found on websites such as Ancestry.com, online since 1996, and 23andMe, founded in 2006.

Like many twenty-first-century people, the author of Matthew's Gospel had an interest in genealogy. It's on full display in today's Gospel as the author traces the forty-two generations from Abraham to Christ. Contemporary readers might be shocked to discover that some of Jesus's relatives had spotty reputations.

Tamar is the first woman mentioned in the genealogy, and she did not have the most reputable character. We find her story in the thirty-eighth chapter of Genesis. After losing two husbands and waiting in vain for Judah to fulfill the promise of his youngest son as a husband, she disguises herself as a prostitute and conceives twin sons with Judah.

A second relative of Jesus is Rahab. Her story is told in the Book of Joshua, chapter 2. She became a part of Israel after hiding two Israelite spies from the authorities of Jericho. She was a prostitute.

Ruth is another relative. The Book of Ruth is named for this Moabite woman who committed herself to the Israelite people by an oath. She was a sexually forward woman.

Bathsheba (not mentioned by name but referred to as "the wife of Uriah") and David are mentioned. David was a murderer who had Uriah killed after committing adultery with Bathsheba.

Why didn't the evangelist obliterate the memories of such people to preserve Jesus's dignity and divinity? Perhaps he wanted to highlight that Jesus is truly human, with shady relatives who had skeletons in their closets.

PONDER

- What relatives do I hesitate to embrace because I consider them sinners?
- What does the story of David say about God's love beyond all telling?

DECEMBER 18

Love Before Logic: Matthew 1:18–25

Richard was a senior manager for a major accounting firm. Hearing of the need for an executive director of an inner-city math program for disadvantaged students, he resigned from the accounting firm and accepted the director's job with a substantial pay cut. When questioned, he simply told his friends he had to "trust his gut."

Karen's oldest son had dropped out of college and spent four years hopping from job to job. He was clearly depressed and trying to find himself. When he asked to return home to live, Karen's husband was adamantly opposed to what he called an "irrational request." Karen, however, kept insisting that sometimes "love has to come before logic."

In today's Gospel, we find Joseph in one of those predicaments that raises struggles between the head and the heart. He discovers that his fiancée is pregnant, and he certainly is not the child's father. Because he was a righteous man, he had decided to do the logical thing—to quietly divorce Mary, and yet, based on a dream, he makes an extraordinary decision of love beyond all telling that goes against common sense. He changed his mind and decided to take Mary into his home as his wife. Because he never speaks a word in the Scriptures, we can only wonder if or how Joseph might have justified his decision to family and friends.

We sometimes find ourselves at a crossroads that demands a deliberate choice between the head or the heart. Such moments in our lives make us only too aware that life is never black or white; rather, it is usually filled with gray. It is in these agonizing moments that we can look to the example of St. Joseph and realize that common sense and logic sometimes are paradoxically irrational before the mystery of life, the manifestation of love beyond all telling. Indeed, as the philosopher Blaise Pascal once remarked, there are times in our lives when the heart has its reasons about which reason itself knows nothing.

PONDER

- At the major crossroads in my life, did I favor the head or the heart? What was the outcome?
- In what situations or circumstances do I find myself struggling with the "gray areas" of life?

DECEMBER 19

Overcoming Doubts: Luke 1:5–25

I remember growing up in New Orleans and one day telling my mother that I wanted to go to China. "Go in the backyard and start digging, Albert, and sooner or later, you'll get there," was her response. I tried but gave up after a few hours. I needed more iced tea and a bigger shovel.

In 1990, the Franciscan Order requested volunteers to study the Chinese language and culture and then find a way to bring the Franciscan presence back to mainland China. My heart skipped a beat as I read the letter and realized I had the opportunity to fulfill a childhood dream. But after my initial enthusiasm, reality began to set in with all its accompanying fears and self-doubts. Did I really have what it takes to be a foreign missionary? Did I have the ability to learn a language as difficult as Chinese? What would happen if I realized I had made a mistake—would I have the humility to return to the United States? How would that affect my reputation among the friars? Would I be considered a failure? I spent the latter half of 1990 and the first half of 1991 beating my head against the brick wall built by fears and self-doubts.

In today's Gospel, Gabriel, the messenger from God, tells Zechariah not to fear and that God would accomplish a marvelous act in his and his wife's lives. Indeed, in their old age, Zechariah and Elizabeth would become parents and have a son. Zechariah is dumbfounded and momentarily questions the power of God. He is consequently made speechless for this initial lack of faith. Doubts are audacious when it comes to what God can do.

God is constantly trying to stretch us and call us beyond our fears and self-doubts. Indeed, where the grace of God calls us, the grace of God will keep us. And sometimes, we fail to realize that the paths down which God summons us lead us, in fact, to the realization of our deepest hopes and dreams. But our challenge, like Zechariah's, is to break through our fears and doubts and trust God, who reveals to us, time and again, the multifaceted dimensions of a love beyond all telling.

PONDER

- What fears and self-doubts are currently hindering me from responding to the call of God in my life?
- What experiences in my life give witness to the fact that God can be trusted to help me overcome my fears and doubts?

DECEMBER 20

Believing in Angels: Luke 1:26–38

A small angel sitting on a birdbath in Tony and Marcia's front yard greets you. A small sign over their doorbell reads, "We believe in angels." When you enter their house, you will see a porcelain angel with big wings and a flowing robe hovering over their fireplace. And then there are the angel coffee mugs, and the candle fashioned in the form of an angel.

I once asked Marcia the reason behind all these figurines. "They remind Tony and me not to become so absorbed in our chores that we fail to see an angel sent by God." I couldn't help but call to remind the belief of the Hasidic Jews: angels enter our lives one hundred times a day. The challenge in life is to recognize every single one of them.

From the Hasidic point of view, the amazing thing about today's Gospel is not that the archangel Gabriel entered Mary's life; rather, the amazing thing was that Mary recognized this moment as an annunciation from God and responded with a "Yes! Let it be!" that instantly took on flesh within her womb. And she bore that incarnate Son of God and longed for him with a love beyond all telling.

In the Catholic tradition, Mary holds a privileged place of love and devotion. She stands within the Church as a great contemplative who was wide awake. With eyes wide open, she understood that each person she encountered was a messenger of God—and her attentive response to each was an expression of her life as a handmaid of the Lord. With such an attitude, she discovered the annunciations of daily life and the incarnation of a lifetime.

It's easy to become so absorbed in our own agendas, plans, and projects that we lose sight of what the nineteenth-century spiritual classic *Abandonment to Divine Providence* calls "the sacrament of the present moment." Every hour of the day God is sending angels into our lives who ask us to respond to their needs, their requests, and their love. Are our eyes open to recognize these annunciations? Are our hearts prepared to respond to them?

Annunciations are so frequent; incarnations are so rare.

PONDER

- Who have been the angels God sent into my life today? How did I respond to them?
- When was the last time someone made me feel like an angel by treating me with attention, care, and concern?

DECEMBER 21

A Leap for Joy: Luke 1:39–45

"Thanks so much for the talk. You will never know how helpful it was. For the past three months, I have been riddled with guilt over George's suicide. I keep telling myself that I should have seen the signs, that I should have sensed his depression. I'm so grateful for your help."

As I returned the note to the envelope, I couldn't help but remember my father's death by suicide. I carried its pain for many years. And over the years, almost imperceptibly, God helped me to move beyond the guilt. Indeed, my father's death took on a life of its own within me and now, once again, some forty years after his death, I found his death giving life to another person left behind by suicide.

Of all the Gospel scenes, today's is truly unique because the main characters are two pregnant women. Mary and Elizabeth's visit is a celebration of God's miracle in each of their lives: one, a young virgin, now bears a human life within herself; the other, beyond childbearing years, also bears a life of her own. One life will prepare the way for the other. The two women did not realize that this visitation possessed a richness and fullness that would ultimately change the world as salvation history, and God's love beyond all telling, unfolded within their wombs.

What we carry within ourselves can make a real difference in the lives of others. We rarely know what others carry within. Sometimes it's a message that encourages us to continue walking the path of life, and sometimes it's a need that we can address to help the other. In either case, because of God's mysterious way of bringing people to us in a sacred moment of history, two people meet and a richness and fullness blossom that makes one person leap for you. It is precisely for this reason that we should daily ponder within our hearts, the life—needy or full as it might be—

that is growing within so that we might be receptive to the grace of visitation.

PONDER

- What life is growing inside of me? How can it help others? How can others help me bring it to birth?
- When was my last moment of visitation? How did this encounter change me or the other person?

DECEMBER 22

Golden Threads: Luke 1:46–56

Marge was in her late seventies. She knew her life was coming to an end, and I felt honored that she had requested that I come to anoint her in the hospital. After celebrating the sacrament of the anointing of the sick, I asked her how she felt looking back on her long life.

"Well, one thing is for certain: it was filled with lots of twists and turns which never left me with a dull moment. What I expected to happen didn't; and what did happen, I could never have predicted in a million years. But God was with me amid all the surprises and struggles, and as I look back on my seventy-seven years, I have a sense that I was part of a bigger plan."

Marge paused and added, "I am filled with so much gratitude. It's amazing to see what happens when you get out of God's way."

Those sentiments expressed by Marge at the end of her long life are reflected in Mary's proclamation of praise today as she reflects on God's action in her young life. She prays in joy and awe of God's gracious and generous action in the small and big events of life: from singling her out with attentive love as a servant, to the surprises of scattering the proud, lifting up the lowly, providing for the hungry, and coming to the help of the chosen people. In each case, God has taken the initiative. Mary is consciously aware that he whom she bears and longs for with a love beyond all telling is irreplaceable in the larger dream and promise of God's love toward creation.

Hindsight is always 20/20, as the saying goes. When we reflect on the events of our own lives, we discover that amid all our disappointments and joys, God is at work, carefully, tenderly, and deliberately weaving the tapestry of salvation history in which Mary, Marge, you, and I are golden threads.

PONDER

- How was God at work in the disappointments of my life? In the joys of my life?
- What role has God called me to play in the history of salvation?

DECEMBER 23

God's Grace on Parade: Luke 1:57–66

Shirley was distraught. She had taken off her wedding ring to do some gardening and when she went to put it back on, she couldn't find it. It had seemingly vanished and was missing for over two months. A friend gave her some traditional advice, "Pray to St. Anthony. If anyone can find it, he surely can." She prayed daily and within one week, her wedding ring was back on her finger. Shirley goes to Mass every Tuesday now to thank God.

Maria and Gilberto had tried with no success for seven years to have a child. They started praying nightly to Our Lady of Guadalupe, asking her help so that they might be able to accept this disappointment. Their disappointment was turned into ecstatic joy when little Juan was born. Now, every year, they celebrate Juan's age in the number of roses they present to Our Lady of Guadalupe on December 12.

The Advent season commemorates and celebrates the miracles of God, both past and present. In today's Gospel, we hear what God accomplished in the lives of Elizabeth and Zechariah. At an advanced age they have a son. And the name they choose for their son is recognition of the miraculous nature of the event. The Hebrew name John literally means "the gift of God." Recognizing and naming the miracle in their lives frees the tongue of one to bless God and causes others to ponder their own lives and hearts.

Someone has described miracles as "God's grace on parade." Indeed, they are! They come in small incidents, like finding a lost wedding ring, and big events, like having a baby, and they are stunning witnesses to the power and action of God in our ordinary lives. Recognizing them requires the daily habit of reflecting on and pondering the experiences our hearts treasure. In the tradition of Elizabeth and Zechariah, Shirley, Maria and Gilberto, by naming them as miracles, our mouths are opened and our tongues are loosened to proclaim that God's love beyond all telling is alive and well—and walking the streets!

PONDER

- What have been the miracles that God has accomplished in my life? How have I named them and proclaimed them to others?
- What can I do on a practical basis to remember and commemorate the miracles God has accomplished for me?

DECEMBER 24: THE MORNING MASS

Praise Breaks Forth from Silence: Luke 1:67–79

Many years ago, I made a ten-day contemplative prayer retreat at a Trappist monastery with thirty other people. We sat together in silent prayer five times a day, each session lasting one hour. Each of us had signed a commitment not to talk during the entire ten days.

I still remember returning to my community at the end of the ten days. The friars kept teasing me, "Albert, you've been silent for ten days and now you just can't shut up! It's as if you are making up for lost time." The friars hit the nail on the head. I just couldn't keep quiet about what I had learned and experienced during the ten days of silence.

Because he doubted the words of Gabriel, Zechariah was unable to speak for nine months. One can only wonder if those nine months of silence gave him cause to pause and ponder the meaning of his future son's birth. He no doubt had time to reflect on the name the archangel Gabriel said to give the child—the Hebrew *Yochanan*, meaning "God is gracious." That name not only captured the miraculous birth to Elizabeth and Zechariah but also the role their son would play in the history of God's love beyond all telling.

On the eighth day, the parents brought John to be circumcised. Suddenly, Zechariah's silence came to an end, his tongue was loosened and filled with the Holy Spirit; nine months of prayerful reflection poured out of him. He prophesied in a beautiful hymn that some scholars believe may have been a Jewish Christian hymn of praise that Luke placed on the lips of Zechariah.

The hymn, containing rich Old Testament imagery, highlights the relationship between John and Jesus. The first half of the hymn sings of Jesus as a "mighty Savior," promised by former prophets, and the fulfillment of God's ancient covenant. The second half turns to John and proclaims him "the prophet of the Most High" who will prepare both the way for the Savior and the hearts of the people. The hymn concludes with reference to God's mercy, light, life, and desire for peace: "In the tender compassion of our God the dawn from on high shall break upon us, to shine on those who dwell in darkness and the shadow of death, and to guide our feet into the way of peace."

This hymn captures the essence of Advent and thus provides a most fitting conclusion to the season.

PONDER

- When did my silence break forth into a hymn of praise like Zechariah's?
- How does Zechariah's hymn speak to my experiences of the spiritual life?

The Christmas Season

THE NATIVITY OF THE LORD: VIGIL MASS, YEARS A, B, AND C

The Good, the Bad, and the Ugly, and Love Before Logic: Matthew 1:1–25

See the reflections and questions for December 17 and 18.

THE NATIVITY OF THE LORD: MASS DURING THE NIGHT, YEARS A, B, AND C

Become What You Love: Luke 2:1–14

Gertrude and Joseph have been married for a little over fifty years. These years have taught Joseph the exact size of a "pinch" of sugar for Gerti's morning coffee, and he himself has come to appreciate the same. Five decades have taught Gertrude the joys of a monthly trip to the library, something she learned to enjoy from Joe while they were still dating in college. Gertrude claims Joe taught her that cute way of smiling when answering the phone; Joseph says he picked up the habit from Gerti.

Gertrude's and Joseph's acquired habits speak volumes about how love transforms two people into one. They also give us an important insight into today's feast: you become what you love.

The Christian tradition has usually spoken of Christmas as God's response to human sinfulness. Adam and Eve disobeyed God and ate the fruit of the forbidden tree; God, in an act of divine generosity, sent his Son as a sacrifice to right the wrong of our first parents. Christmas began a worthy act of obedience to outweigh the first act of disobedience.

The Franciscan tradition has sung very differently about the Child of the crib. In the fourteenth century, Blessed John Duns Scotus stated that God intended to share the depths of his divine being from all eternity. Indeed, even if Adam and Eve had not sinned in the Garden of Eden, Christ still would have been born. Why? Because God fell head over heels in love with us and wanted to experience and transform the depths of our humanity. Human sinfulness did not create the need for Christmas—love did! That first cry that filled the lungs of the Babe of Bethlehem proclaims that God finds you and me utterly adorable and lovable. You become what you love.

Mary bore the Son in her womb and longed for him with a love beyond all telling. Today, we discover that the Son whom the Virgin bore is, in fact, God's love beyond all telling.

PONDER

- What personal qualities and gifts does God find utterly adorable and lovable in me?
- "You become what you love"—how has love for God transformed me and the way I live?

THE NATIVITY OF THE LORD: MASS AT DAWN, YEARS A, B, AND C

The "Thing" of Christmas: Luke 2:15–20

Roughly 20 percent of the world's population speaks English—that's about 1.5 billion people. It is often adopted as the lingua franca between nonnative speakers. Such speakers soon discover that a word in their native language is so subtle, unique, and culturally bound that English doesn't have an equivalent. For example, the Japanese word *datsuzoku* means to escape from the daily routine, to take a break from the conventions and mundanities of one's life, to discover more creativity, resourcefulness, and to perceive your surroundings differently. *Hygge* in Danish suggests a strong feeling of coziness, alone or with others, when a person feels content, secure, and comforted; it can also refer to a ritualistic aspect of your life that brings comfort, such as making a cup of coffee every morning. The Italian word *abbiocco* describes the sleepy, contented feeling that comes after eating a big meal. In effect, some feelings or experiences just don't translate into one word.

On the other hand, some languages are imprecise and have a catchall word for many things. For example, the Chinese word *shiqing* ("thing") has a multipurpose use. It can refer to a situation, circumstance, affair, or an incomprehensible matter. It's used in the translation of the shepherds' statement from today's Gospel, "Let us go, then, to Bethlehem to see this thing that has taken place, which the Lord has made known to us."

A pious person might think that it's disrespectful or even scandalous to refer to the birth of the Son of God as a "thing." However, incomprehensible and inconceivable as the birth is, "thing" might be an apt descriptor. It reminds us that what Mary longed for with love beyond all telling was incarnate in the Babe of Bethlehem. That reality is so ineffable that human language is constrained. Indeed, our words and images stagger, wobble, and stumble because none of them can accurately describe this unfathomable and incomprehensible miracle of divinity made humanity. In the words of the French novelist and essayist Léon Bloy, "When those who love God try to talk about Him, their words are blind lions looking for springs in the desert."

PONDER

- What word or image or Christmas song captures the mystery of the Incarnation for me?
- In what circumstances do I experience the inadequacy of human language?

THE NATIVITY OF THE LORD: MASS DURING THE DAY, YEARS A, B, AND C

A Worthy Prologue: John 1:1–18

Anyone who has majored in English literature will tell you how important a prologue can be. The fourteen opening lines of William Shakespeare's *Romeo and Juliet* are considered one of the most famous prologues in English literature as they succinctly establish the setting, conflict, and feud between the Capulet and Montague families. Even those who have not majored in literature will recognize the opening lines of *A Tale of Two Cities* by Charles Dickens ("It was the best of times, it was the worst of times...") as they are the most quoted lines from the book.

Like the succinct summary found in *Romeo and Juliet*'s prologue and the famous opening line of *A Tale of Two Cities*, John's Prologue offers a succinct summary of the Fourth Gospel's major themes and a famous opening line. Some of the eighteen lines of the Prologue might have been an early Christian hymn—or maybe even a non-Christian hymn that has been "baptized" by the author. Displaying deep thought and echoing philosophical ideas, the Prologue begins with the famous words, "In the beginning was the Word," evoking the beginning of Genesis and situating the ministry of Jesus within all human history and even beyond it before the beginning of time. The Word is not simply speech or a power that God can use to create. The Word became known in a person, Jesus. Through the Word, God creates and sustains the world and guides human beings.

One scholar has insightfully compared the Prologue to "waves" on the seashore. There is a statement and a restatement of the same basic truths about God's action in and through Jesus Christ that deepen as the "wave" runs farther up the shore. He notes a threefold structure to the Prologue: the announcement, description, and revelation of the eternal Word (verses 1–5); the ministry of John the Baptist and the response, both negatively and positively, of human beings to the presence of the Word and the transformative power of faith in the Word (verses 6–13); the Word and the divine glory manifested in the incarnation (literally, "pitching his tent" among us) (verses 14–18).

As contemporary readers allow the threefold waves of the Prologue with its stark contrasts between light and darkness, the world above and the world below, to wash over them, they will get a sense of the profound ineffable mystery of God's love beyond all telling that takes on flesh and blood on this Christmas Day.

PONDER

- What is my initial reaction to the Prologue of John's Gospel?
- As I ponder and pray over John's Prologue, what line or lines touch my heart?

DECEMBER 26: FEAST OF ST. STEPHEN

The Crib and the Cross: Matthew 10:17–22

The Christmas holidays often give rise to nostalgia and sentimentality. Christmas trees, mistletoe, eggnog, wrapping paper strewn all over the floor, and nativity scenes adorned with lights all have ways of stirring thoughts of Christmases past. Although these days cause some people to slip into the "holiday blues," most of us smile and chuckle to ourselves as we recall our first kiss under the mistletoe, our first sip of eggnog, and the disappointment we felt when we were bypassed for the role as a member of the Holy Family in the grammar school Christmas pageant.

Today's feast is intended to shock us and jolt us out of any sentimentality about the birthday of the Babe of Bethlehem. We remember the death of the first martyr of the faith, Stephen. Filled with wisdom and passion for the teachings of Jesus, Stephen defended his faith before the Sanhedrin when trumped-up charges were presented by false witnesses. This passionate defense so infuriated his listeners that they led Stephen out of the city and stoned him to death. A role model for believers, Stephen is portrayed as dying with words similar to the Crucified's on his lips, "Receive my spirit" (Acts 7:59, from the first reading).

The Gospel speaks of the challenge of being a witness for Jesus and the inevitable suffering that will result. Jesus speaks of persecutions, family betrayal, hatred, and even death for those who remain faithful to him. Jesus promises the gifts of the Holy Spirit and salvation for those who remain steadfast in their witness.

Today's feast starkly and boldly insists that Christmas isn't just kid stuff; rather, we are reminded that the splendor of the crib is shrouded with the shadow of the cross. The story of God's love beyond all telling is a very adult affair that demands, in the spirit of the martyr St. Stephen, a commitment of one's passion and life.

PONDER

- How do I feel when I reflect on the manager of Bethlehem being overshadowed by the cross of Calvary? What do the crib and cross say to me?
- How do my actions show that faith in Jesus is not merely an intellectual affair but a fundamental commitment of my passion and my life?

DECEMBER 27: FEAST OF ST. JOHN, APOSTLE AND EVANGELIST

The Disciple Whom Jesus Loved: John 20:1a, 2–8

Today, we celebrate the Feast of St. John the apostle and evangelist. Although biblical scholars seriously doubt that the "other disciple whom Jesus loved" mentioned in today's Gospel is the same person as John the apostle and evangelist, tradition has linked them together as one and the same based on a concluding remark found in the Gospel of John (see John 21:24).

The disciple whom Jesus loved certainly stands out prominently in the Fourth Gospel. He reclines in the place of honor, immediately next to Jesus, at the Last Supper (see John 13:23). He follows the arrested Jesus to the courtyard of Annas the high priest (see John 18:15). Among the followers who were not afraid or embarrassed to stand at the foot of the cross, he is the only male; no doubt it was his fidelity that motivated the dying Jesus to entrust Mary, his mother, to that disciple's care (see John 19:26–27). Of the first three followers to see the empty tomb, it is written only of him that "he saw and believed." When the risen Jesus reveals himself to seven disciples at the Sea of Tiberias, the disciple whom Jesus loved first recognizes his friend and exclaims to Peter, "It is the Lord!" (see John 21:7). The very reference, "the disciple whom Jesus loved," clearly suggests a special and unique bond of friendship and intimacy shared between the two—and his actions during the final days of Jesus's earthly life speak volumes about its reality.

Each culture and ethnicity have its own unique expressions and rituals for friendship. However, despite the differences, there are surprisingly universal qualities of those we call "friend." Friends are faithful. They believe in us when others might doubt. They are entrusted with our treasures, stories, opinions, and memories. They are the first to recognize us by voice or visage. Indeed, friendship is one of the ordinary ways that God touches our lives, brings us to life, and gives us a glimpse into an extraordinary love beyond all telling.

PONDER

- What are some practical ways that I express my fidelity, faith, and commitment to those who have graced me with the gift of friendship?
- What have I learned about God's love for me through the friends God has sent into my life?

DECEMBER 28: FEAST OF THE HOLY INNOCENTS, MARTYRS

Recognizing Hungers and Obsessions: Matthew 2:13–18

Self-esteem and healthy pride are important to have a realistic sense of self. They give us the ability to set appropriate boundaries and be poised and confident in what we say and do. They foster a spirit of adventure by opening us up to the new and unknown. They help us develop the facility to acknowledge and compliment others' talents and accomplishments. Self-esteem and pride protect us from viewing anyone else as a threat.

Without self-esteem and pride, however, we become needy, defensive, and suspicious, living each day cowering like a punished puppy or barking our way through the week with endless justifications and demands. Sometimes we might thrust ourselves on others, becoming aggressive, difficult, and cruel. All of this betrays our paranoia, the obsession to look over our shoulders, to constantly compare ourselves to others, and to frequently feel threatened.

Today's Gospel highlights just how far someone lacking self-esteem and pride will go. As tragic as it sounds, Herod is clearly threatened by the birth of a newborn baby announced by the Magi. Unsure of the exact time of his birth, Herod slaughters all boys two years old or younger in the town of Bethlehem and its vicinity. Clearly, he wants to wipe out any future competition that could potentially threaten his authority and control of the people. His lust for power is as appalling as the deaths of the innocent boys.

The Feast of the Holy Innocents challenges us to take a hard, honest look at ourselves and ask what the hungers and obsessions in our life are for which we are willing to slaughter the reputation, career, or potential of another. It is so easy to victimize others for the sake of our pride, our position in the office, our need to bask alone in the prestige or publicity of the moment, our craving for popularity or pleasure. Like Herod, we continue to think that the world should revolve around us.

PONDER

- In what areas of my life do I lack self-confidence or feel threatened by others?
- What innocents have I victimized in my own life?

DECEMBER 29: FIFTH DAY IN THE OCTAVE OF THE NATIVITY OF THE LORD

Hopes and Dreams: Luke 2:22–35

Kathy is a single parent and Chinese immigrant. After earning a high school equivalency diploma, she had hopes of earning a two-year associate's degree. However, she decided to forego her dream and send her son to college. She cleaned hotel rooms by day and served as a waitress in a neighborhood restaurant by night. Life wasn't easy.

Tears trickled down her cheeks when her son, in cap and gown, walked across the stage to receive his bachelor's degree. Those late nights coming home, the arguments over homework, the embarrassment over her poor English when talking to teachers suddenly blossomed into a dream come true. She froze in her seat when the president of the small college allowed her son, as prearranged, to briefly address the commencement ceremony.

Her son said, "Mom, thank you for this gift. I hope one day to help you with your dream." Spoken in almost fluent Chinese, it was a public promise that only the two could understand.

Years later, Kathy was attending the same college, thanks to her son's financial support, and on the verge of completing her bachelor's degree.

Simeon, too, had a dream. He lived his entire life waiting to see the promised Messiah. That wait came to an end in today's Gospel as he held the infant Christ and praised God for a promised fulfilled.

Hopes and dreams fuel our stamina to endure sacrifices, detours, difficult times, and inconveniences. Some people, like Kathy, are lucky enough to have their hopes fulfilled early on. Others, like Simeon, must wait a lifetime to witness a dream come true.

And still others go through life bearing the sorrow of shattered hopes and deflated dreams.

Realized, unfulfilled, or deflated, hopes and dreams nonetheless remind us that there is an insatiable hunger deep within the human heart. They point to a life that is bigger, better, and brighter. Indeed, our hopes and dreams are simply echoes and reminders of the one thing that will satisfy us—God's divine love beyond all telling that we celebrate during this season.

PONDER

- What are my hopes and dreams? What do they say about me and my values?
- What hopes of mine have been shattered? What dreams of mine are deflated?

DECEMBER 30: SIXTH DAY IN THE OCTAVE OF THE NATIVITY OF THE LORD

Living Prayers: Luke 2:36–40

My grandmother lived as a widow for over fifteen years. I can still see the stack of prayer books and the rosary that she kept on top of her Bible and in front of the television set. Morning and evening would find her "reading my prayers" or "praying the rosary." But Gram was certainly not a prayer factory or a rote pray-er. Her prayers spilled over into the way she would meticulously prepare her famous oven-barbecued chicken for me and then allow me to dip pieces of French bread in the drippings at the bottom of the pan. As I ate, she would talk about simple things: the wonder of the rose bushes; how she feared that "old man Stein," the neighbor across the street, might be sick; her worries about her two daughters; her gratitude for her grandchildren. Only now, as an adult, do I realize that her musings and conversations betrayed the content of her prayers. Indeed, over the years of fingering rosaries and turning worn-out prayer book pages, this woman had herself become a living prayer of wonder, gratitude, and intercession.

We meet the elderly Anna in today's Gospel. She, too, spent her final years as a widow of prayer—"she never left the temple, but worshiped night and day with fasting and prayer." Her seventy-seven years of prayers had not only transformed her into a prophetess but also had changed the way she lived her life: her prayers had made her prayerful, aware, and awake. She is compelled to step forward and speak about the child when he was brought into the temple. She gave praise and thanks to God while testifying to those awaiting the redemption of Jerusalem.

In retirement villages, nursing homes, and assisted-living facilities throughout the world, there are hundreds of pious widows and widowers. Having spent decades attending church services and time in prayer, these men and women have been transformed like my grandmother and Anna into living prayers. Their prayers have made them prayerful. Having nurtured and nourished God's Word, they themselves have become living sacraments and symbols of God's love beyond all telling.

PONDER

- Among my extended family and friends, who has become a living prayer and sacrament of God's love?
- How do I maintain fidelity to daily prayer in my busy, hectic life? What challenges does daily prayer present to me?

DECEMBER 31: SEVENTH DAY IN THE OCTAVE OF THE NATIVITY OF THE LORD

A Worthy Prologue: John 1:1–18

See the reflection and questions for the Nativity of the Lord: Mass During the Day, Years A, B, and C.

FEAST OF THE HOLY FAMILY OF JESUS, MARY, AND JOSEPH, YEAR A

Looking for a Home: Matthew 2:13–15, 19–23

Sister Norma Pimentel, a Missionary of Jesus and executive director of Catholic Charities of the Rio Grande Valley, was named by *Time* magazine as one of "The 100 Most Influential People of 2020." To this day, she continues to support migrants who are seeking refuge along Texas's border with Mexico. With sleeves rolled up and many helpful volunteers, she provides shelter, food, clothing, and comfort to those seeking a better life. In his *Time* tribute to her, Julián Castro, former U.S. Secretary of Housing and Urban Development, offered blistering criticism of the then-current presidential administration: "[Sister Norma's] work has taken on greater importance in the era of Donald Trump, and for good reason. As he has acted with cruelty toward migrants, she has acted with compassion. As he has preyed on the vulnerable and sought rejection, she has preached community and acceptance. As he has promoted fear, she has taught love."

That tension between heartless politics and compassionate love is on full display in today's Gospel. Herod was intent on killing the Babe of Bethlehem and so Joseph, once again following the advice of an angel in a dream, endured the inconvenience and challenges of uprooting his family under cover of night and became immigrants to Egypt, not knowing its language and unfamiliar with its customs. At the death of Herod, Joseph was instructed to take his family back to Israel. Hesitant because Herod's son was now ruling Judea, Joseph chose the region of Galilee and settled in Nazareth. Like contemporary migrants, Jesus, Mary, and Joseph knew only too well the challenges of building a safe and protective home.

Today's Gospel might be disconcerting to some people who think that a political agenda is the privileged arena where the divine will is manifested. Even more disconcerting is the implication that God is not found in the corridors of power and prestige but on the periphery where people struggle for basic necessities such as shelter, food, clothing, and comfort. The Christmas season reminds us that God is found off the beaten track—in towns like Bethlehem and places like migrant shelters.

PONDER

- Why does the Bible always highlight God's favor toward refugees, immigrants, and the disadvantaged? What are my thoughts and feelings about that?
- How do I understand the refugee and immigration crisis in light of the Gospel's and the Church's call for justice and peace?

FEAST OF THE HOLY FAMILY OF JESUS, MARY, AND JOSEPH, YEAR B

Hopes and Dreams and Living Prayers: Luke 2:22–40

See the reflections and questions for December 29 and 30.

FEAST OF THE HOLY FAMILY OF JESUS, MARY, AND JOSEPH, YEAR C

Purpose and Mission: Luke 2:41–52

After my ordination to the priesthood, my mother and I walked side-by-side to the church hall for the reception where I would offer my first priestly blessing to those who approached me. As we walked, my mother suddenly turned around and stood in front of me. I stopped in my tracks. "Sugar Pie," she said, using her favorite pet name for me, "I always knew you were going to be a priest." My look of disbelief urged her on. "Did you know that you were born on Holy Thursday, 1955? I still remember you came out of my womb, the doctor slapped your bare bottom, you gasped, and then exclaimed, 'Let us begin. In the name of the Father, and of the Son, and of the Holy Spirit.'" While chuckling over my mother's vivid imagination, I was flooded with memories of growing up and playing priest. I still remember the day I invested in a thin stole used to hear confessions and practiced hearing the confession of our dog, Bingo. I can never remember not wanting to be a priest and Franciscan.

Don't think that the evangelist's vivid imagination is on display in today's Gospel, and don't think the evangelist wants to relate a story about a precocious or disobedient twelve-year-old Jesus. Perhaps the evangelist wants to highlight something more important: at an early age Jesus had a growing sense of having a particular mission. His rhetorical question to his parents, "Did you not know that I must be in my Father's house?" suggests a wisdom and sense of purpose far beyond his years.

Each one of us has been given a purpose and mission for the sake of the kingdom by virtue of our baptism. As we grow from childhood through adolescence to adulthood and mature in the faith, we hopefully embrace what can only be described as a higher calling. That calling will be contained in our vocations as single, married, or celibate and will be as unique as our fingerprints. Hopefully, we will not allow worldly allurements such as power, prestige, possessions, pleasure, or praise to distract us from the higher calling given to us by the Father.

PONDER

- What is my purpose and mission in this life? When did I become aware of it?
- How comfortable am I with the idea that Jesus only gradually became aware of his identity and mission as we grew from childhood through adolescence to adulthood?

SECOND SUNDAY AFTER THE NATIVITY OF THE LORD

A Worthy Prologue: John 1:1–18

See the reflection and questions for the Nativity of the Lord, Mass During the Day, Years A, B, and C.

JANUARY 1: SOLEMNITY OF MARY, MOTHER OF GOD

Being Mothers of Christ: Luke 2:16–21

"What's your New Year's resolution?" It's the question that some people might ask of us today. As we welcome another year, many of us will make decisions in our lives that we've kept postponing: to quit smoking, reconcile with an alienated friend or family member, go on a diet, get involved with a local soup kitchen, visit an elderly relative on a regular basis, deepen our awareness of global issues, be more truthful with the boss, attend Mass during the week, or develop a hobby. The possibilities are endless.

On this day when we choose a resolution, the Church commemorates the Virgin Mary under the title which speaks of her vocation and privileged place in salvation history: Mother of God. This is one of the most ancient titles for Mary and, surprisingly, was not without controversy. When Nestorius, a fifth-century heretic, questioned its appropriateness, the Council of Ephesus in 431 reaffirmed its validity. Mary is the disciple of her Son par excellence. Her vocation was to listen intently to God's Word, to surrender to the vocation of motherhood despite the fears and doubts it raised within her, long for her Son with love beyond all telling, and ultimately to give birth to divine love made flesh.

And yet what Mary did is the call and challenge of every Christian. St. Francis of Assisi, in a letter to all Christian believers, insightfully wrote, "We are mothers when we carry Him in our heart and body through a divine love and a pure and sincere conscience and give birth to Him through a holy activity which must shine as an example before others." Indeed, our motherhood of Christ, like the Virgin's, consists in bearing the love of God within our hearts and then giving birth to that love by the way we live our lives.

As we welcome another year, it's important that we affirm

our vocation, by whatever New Year's resolution we adopt, to being mothers of Christ in imitation of Mary, the Mother of God.

PONDER

- How does my New Year's resolution reflect the call and challenge to give birth to Christ?
- What are practical ways in which I can identify with Mary, the Mother of God?

WEEKDAYS OF CHRISTMASTIME: FROM JANUARY 2 TO THE SATURDAY BEFORE THE FEAST OF THE BAPTISM OF THE LORD

MONDAY, TUESDAY, WEDNESDAY, THURSDAY, FRIDAY, AND SATURDAY

Beyond Titles and Positions: John 1:19–28

The People's Republic of China forbids foreign missionaries from residing within the borders of the mainland. And so, for twelve years, I had to have a secular job to live there legally. As a Franciscan missionary, I was a college professor, a director of human resources for an international accounting firm, and a human resources consultant.

I was often asked by friars, family, and friends, "How can you justify being a missionary and working these secular jobs?" Many could not understand my reminder that the Franciscan missionary vocation is first and foremost a ministry of presence.

The priests and Levites in today's Gospel were trying to understand the role of John the Baptist. He patiently denied being the Christ, Elijah, or the Prophet. They pressed him, asking, "What do you have to say for yourself?" Leaping beyond titles and positions, he declared, "I am the voice of one crying out in the desert, 'Make straight the way of the Lord.'"

It's so easy to get caught up in being called "Doctor Matthews" or "Sister Monica." It's so tempting to define or describe ourselves by our occupations as CEOs, construction workers, web designers, or teachers. And yet the question posed in the Gospel—"What do you have to say for yourself?"—challenges us to look beyond our roles, titles, and occupations. It can be threatening because it's not asking, "Who are you?" It's more like a disarming, "Who do you think you are?"

That question exposes the interior fire that inflames our desires and drives us to do the things that we do. The brightness of that fire betrays our zeal for life, and its intensity shows the depth of our passion. Some people blaze with self-assurance and radiate an assertiveness and self-confidence that show they are animated by something far greater than a mere career. Indeed, they have a calling, a purpose, a mission that belies any simplistic categorization by title, position, or occupation. Their very presence, words, and deeds all proclaim that they have been sent to pave the way and light the path for others to experience love beyond all telling.

PONDER

- What do I have to say for myself? What is my mission and calling?
- What is more important to me, titles or my life's purpose? How do I allow the former to influence and become an obstacle to the latter?

WEEKDAYS OF CHRISTMASTIME: FROM JANUARY 2 TO THE EPIPHANY OF THE LORD

JANUARY 2

Beyond Titles and Positions: John 1:19–28

See the reflection and questions for Weekdays of Christmastime: From January 2 to the Saturday Before the Feast of the Baptism of the Lord, Monday, Tuesday, Wednesday, Thursday, Friday, and Saturday.

JANUARY 3

Taking the Initiative: John 1:29–34

She went to daily Mass and always prayed a rosary afterward. Every other Saturday afternoon found her waiting in line for confession. She was a pious, good woman. However, her prayers and spiritual practices were her way of doing penance for a sin she had committed some fifty years ago.

Her eyes welled up with tears as the priest reminded her that it was impossible to earn the forgiveness of God. "Jesus takes all our sins away by drenching them in the loving mercy of His Father. God forgives us not because we are good, but because God is good."

John the Baptist is the last of the Old Testament prophets and, as such, provides the "hinge" between the old, Law-based Mosaic covenant and the new, everlasting covenant enfleshed in Jesus. Jews took the initiative for atoning for violations of the Mosaic covenant and went to the temple to offer animal sacrifice. However, in his very life and death, Jesus enfleshes God's initiative that definitively atones for all human sinfulness and now makes any future animal sacrifice useless and unnecessary. Indeed, in today's Gospel, John points to Jesus and says, "Behold, the Lamb of God who takes away the sin of the world." Following Jesus into the new covenant means accepting the reality that a forgiving God takes the lead in continuing and fostering the love affair with humanity.

Of all the aspects of our faith, God's unconditional loving initiative toward us is truly the most mind-boggling. We always try to minimalize the "unconditional" characteristic, saying that God loves us and forgives us "as long as" we are good. Or we think that we must live up to certain requirements to experience God's love and mercy. But the fact is God's love is not some generous return for our acts of piety and charity. It is not payment for services rendered. God loves and forgives us because God is good. That's why this season proclaims a love beyond all telling.

PONDER

- What feelings or thoughts motivate my prayers, Mass attendance, and spiritual practices? Do they place me in the old covenant with Moses or the new covenant with Jesus?
- When was the last time I experienced God taking the initiative and lavishing me with an experience of divine love and mercy? What was my response?

JANUARY 4

The Hole in the Heart: John 1:35–42

Sophia is a people-pleaser. Over the years she has developed the knack for knowing what people need or want. She always tries to honor their wants and wishes in her words and actions. Though she is often perceived as a generous woman who has an uncanny ability to say and do the right thing and sometimes even to contradict herself, those closest to her know differently. Indeed, Sophia's need to please and satisfy others betrays a desperate desire to feel accepted and affirmed by everyone.

Today's Gospel records Jesus asking a simple question of two of John's disciples, "What are you looking for?" Their reply, "Rabbi...where are you staying?", might have arisen from a very practical need. Because the Gospel mentions that it was late in the afternoon, perhaps Andrew and the other disciple were looking for a place to stay to avoid violating the prohibition against travel on the Sabbath.

Typical of John's Gospel, Jesus's question can be heard on a deeper, more provocative level. Perhaps he is asking about the fundamental desire that would satisfy their hearts.

As a result of original sin, we are born with something missing in our lives. Some writers have referred to it as the "hole in the heart." As we mature into adulthood, our culture and upbringing tell us what we need to plug up that hole so we can find apparent happiness. Consequently, we find ourselves chasing after power, prestige, people, possessions, popularity, pleasure, and praise—or something else, thinking such things will cure our heart's restlessness. Unfortunately, it takes us half a lifetime, usually around midlife, to discover that what we seek cannot be found in shopping malls, places of honor, or short-lived infatuations.

Surprisingly, Jesus supplies the answer to the very question he asks. His summons, "Come, and you will see," is an invitation to follow him down life's highways and byways with the poor, the marginalized, the forgotten, and public sinners. Following him as disciples, we experience the truest meaning of love beyond all telling—and the balm that heals the hole in the heart.

PONDER

- What am I truly looking for in life? How has my search been hampered or frustrated?
- How does discipleship to Jesus address my restlessness? What part of Jesus's ministry provides the balm for the hole in my heart?

JANUARY 5

Uprooting Seeds of Narrow-Mindedness: John 1:43–51

At the age of forty-three, he started needing twenty-four-hour nursing care. Suffering with motor neuron disease and amyotrophic lateral sclerosis, confined to a wheelchair, and using a speech synthesizer that allowed him to speak fifteen words a minute, Stephen Hawking proved that Albert Einstein's general theory of relativity implied that space and time had a beginning in the big bang and would have an end in black holes. Hawking was unquestionably the world's leading theoretical physicist.

Born in 1875 to sharecropping parents in Mayesville, South Carolina, Mary McLeod Bethune was the youngest of seventeen children. In her late forties in an old house near the Daytona Beach city dump, she almost single-handedly built what would become Bethune-Cookman College, a school for Blacks who were working on the railroad labor camps of Florida. In 1935, she left Florida for the White House to be an advisor to President Roosevelt.

Ryan Hreljac of Ontario, Canada, has set up a global campaign to dig water wells and supply water pumps for Africa. Today, his foundation has paid for hundreds of wells not only in Africa but also in Central America and South Asia. He started raising money for water wells in 1998 when he was only six years old, resulting in *The Times* of London describing him as "the most successful pre-teen fundraiser on the planet."

When his friend Philip tracked him down and told him that he had found the person written about by Moses and the prophets, Nathanael's first response was, "Can anything good come from Nazareth?" Nathanael's initial response betrays an intolerance—maybe even prejudice—toward people who come from the boondocks.

Nathanael is not alone. The seeds of narrow-mindedness and

intolerance are sown in us because of our background, upbringing, and lack of education. It's so easy to judge others based on their disability, race, age, sexual orientation, or status in life. People like Stephen Hawking, Mary McLeod Bethune, and Ryan Hreljac are reminders that, despite apparent disabilities and disadvantages, everyone has a unique gift from God. Indeed, our talents and abilities all point to God's love beyond all telling.

PONDER

- Who must prove his or her value to me or society? Why?
- When have I been the victim of small-mindedness, prejudice, or bigotry? How did this make me feel?

JANUARY 6

Spiritual Awakenings: Mark 1:7–11 (1st Option)

Michelle's eyes welled up with tears of joy as the nurse handed her the newborn baby for the first time. In that single instant, Michelle realized that her life would be forever changed. From then on, every decision that she and Scott would make would have to take into consideration and include little Aiden. A good place to start would be by going to church on Sundays, something that they had not done since their wedding day two years earlier.

Kathy's birthday gift to David turned out to be exactly what she had hoped it would be for him. Months ahead of time, she had made reservations for him to make a weekend retreat at a Trappist monastery. He jokingly referred to it as his "fishing trip with the monks" until he returned on Sunday night with a newly found interest and desire to continue reading about prayer and the spiritual life. David had discovered something about himself that he had previously not known.

The first option for today's Gospel comes from Mark, and the evangelist suggests that Jesus himself had an awakening at his baptism in the Jordan River. The tearing apart of the skies, the descent of the Spirit in the form of a dove, and the voice resounding from the heavens, "You are my beloved Son," all declare the importance of this event in the life of Jesus. This baptismal experience would immediately plunge Jesus into a wrestling match with Satan in the desert followed by the beginning of his ministry in Galilee. Indeed, his life's mission begins with his baptism in the Jordan.

All of us experience spiritual awakenings. These experiences can be joyful and intriguing as in Michelle's and David's cases. They can also be threatening and confusing as in the death of a loved one or the loss of a job. Moments of awakening give us the freedom to choose whether we want to begin or deepen our relationship with

God. To make the choice for God tears apart the clouds of self-doubt and unbelief to give us the grace to bask in our identity as beloved children of God, as recipients of a love beyond all telling.

PONDER

- When have moments of spiritual awakening occurred in my life? How did I respond to them?
- What specific events in my life have made me bask in being the beloved of God?

JANUARY 6

Jesus, My Ancestor: Luke 3:23–38 (2nd Option)

My first cousin Bruce likes to tell people that, on his father's side of the family, he is a descendant of the infamous nineteenth-century New Orleans pirate, smuggler, and slave trader, Jean Lafitte. The American actor and film producer Matt Damon is a descendant of Richard Warren, one of the pilgrims on the *Mayflower* in the seventeenth century. The actress Angelina Jolie carries French royal blood as a descendant of the early thirteenth-century King Philip II. Megan Markle is a fifth cousin thirteen times removed to the great playwright William Shakespeare. When American actor Edward Norton discovered his twelfth great-grandmother was none other than the Native American woman Pocahontas, he replied, "It makes you realize what a small piece of the human story you are."

Our hearts pump blood through our veins that shares past or present royal lineage, the sufferings of slavery, the pride of conquerors, the joy of pioneers, the creativity of artists, and the ingenuity of explorers. Indeed, as Edward Norton noted, we are all a small piece of a larger human story shaped by our ancestors.

In today's Gospel, Luke highlights the larger human story that rushes through Jesus's veins. He takes a different approach than Matthew, whose Gospel literally begins with the genealogy that highlights Jesus's Jewishness by tracing his lineage through Abraham. Luke's genealogy, on the other hand, is placed differently and has a different purpose. It comes after Jesus's baptism, when his Father declares Jesus the beloved son. Although scholars note that Luke's names do not correspond to the Old Testament genealogies, his interest is in highlighting Jesus's salvific mission to all of humanity. He first notes Jesus's virgin birth by a parenthetical remark ("the son, as was thought, of Joseph") and then traces his ancestors all the way back through pre-Israelite history to one of the parents of all humanity, Adam, and then to God himself.

If we traced the larger human story shaped by our ancestors who were pirates, pilgrims, royalty, authors, and Native Americans and did it through the lens of our faith, we would discover our original parents, Adam and Eve—and suddenly realize that we have an ancestor who is our Savior.

PONDER

- Who among my spiritual ancestors in the faith are important for me? Why?
- How comfortable am I in calling Jesus my ancestor? Why?

JANUARY 7

Having a Good Time: John 2:1–11

In 1910, German theologian and writer, Friedrich Justus Knecht, auxiliary bishop of Freiburg, published his massive book *A Practical Commentary on Holy Scripture*. It received recommendations from fourteen different bishops and went through at least sixteen editions. Although the book is dated by the standards of modern biblical scholarship, it offers three important teachings that emerge from today's Gospel of the wedding feast of Cana.

This first of only seven miracles—called "signs" in the Fourth Gospel—occurred through the intercession of the mother of Jesus and in the presence of his disciples. Mary and the disciples are symbolic of the gathered Church. Mary shows great sensitivity and compassion for the potential embarrassment of the bride and bridegroom and points out the lack of wine to her son. Pointing to him, she tells the servants, "Do whatever he tells you." This is a reminder to twenty-first-century believers that all authentic Marian devotion leads us to the feet of her son, Jesus, and that we should not hesitate to intercede for the potential shame and embarrassment of others.

Second, Knecht points out that this first sign occurs at a wedding feast. This is the scriptural basis for matrimony being one of the seven sacraments, something not shared by our Protestant brothers and sisters. Jesus's presence at the marriage feast is a testament and sign of his sacramental presence when two people become one in marriage. As John will write in one of his letters, "God is love, and those who abide in love abide in God, and God abides in them" (1 John 4:16).

Finally, Jesus likes a good party—and so should we. The belief that Super Bowl celebrations, Mardi Gras carnivals, and retirement parties belong to the "secular realm," as one Catholic commentator recently observed, are just plain silly. Jesus's presence at Cana shows not only that we should rejoice with those who rejoice but also that a good celebration can give us cause to drop to our knees in adoration of God's love beyond all telling.

PONDER

- Does my image of Jesus include him dancing at a party and drinking wine? Why or why not?
- Where do I draw the line between the sacred and the secular?

SUNDAY BETWEEN JANUARY 2 AND JANUARY 8: THE EPIPHANY OF THE LORD, YEARS A, B, C

Room in the Stable: Matthew 2:1–12

When I was a young child, my mother would take me by the hand to the large Christmas crib located next to the sanctuary in the church. Although she would do her best to point out baby Jesus and his mother and father, my attention would naturally gravitate toward the animals in and around the stable. I remember thinking how much fun it was that the church would sometimes look like the Audubon Park Zoo. It's only now as an adult that I see how those animals speak volumes about today's feast.

First, there is the donkey. Lest it go unsaid, it was a very special donkey. According to some stories, that beast of burden had the privilege of carrying the Virgin who longed for her baby with love beyond all telling. Donkeys are not known for their intelligence, and yet we find one near the manager.

Then there are the sheep, brought there by the shepherds who were the first to hear the good news of God's love made flesh. Dirty, smelly, and prone to fleas as they can be, sheep are welcomed inside the stable.

Tradition assigns a camel to each of the three Magi. If you have ever seen a camel at a zoo, you know they have strange humps on their backs and notoriously bad teeth. And yet humps and bad teeth notwithstanding, we usually find three camels in the scene of the manger.

The Feast of the Epiphany manifests the extravagance of God's love beyond all telling: Jesus has come for all peoples, Jew and Gentile alike, as Paul reminds us in the second reading. There are no restrictions or limitations to God's everlasting love. Indeed, if there is room in that stable, around that crib, for a stupid donkey, stinky sheep, and odd-looking camels, there is room in there for the Jew and the Gentile, the saint and the sinner, the intelligent and the ignorant, the flawless and the filthy, the handsome and the homely—for you and for me. God has purposely thrown the doors of the stable wide open so that all may enter and find God's unconditional gifts of love, forgiveness, and peace.

PONDER

- Which person or animal do I identify with the most in the manger scene and why?
- What causes me to hesitate or hinders me from authentically experiencing God's unconditional love?

MONDAY AFTER EPIPHANY (OR JANUARY 7)

Just One Homily: Matthew 4:12–17, 23–25

"Gentleman, let me be very clear," the homiletics professor said to us on the first day of class, "as an ordained person, you will have only one homily, and all your other homilies will be corollaries to this one insight that God has given you and from which you live your life." I took exception to that statement. But now, after more than forty years of priesthood, I see the truth of that statement.

I sometimes think it would be interesting to compile a book called *Sermons Off the Mount*. It would be the one homily that famous and not so famous nonordained people would preach if given the opportunity. Indeed, everyone has one insight about God and the spiritual life that they have learned over the years and out of which their life has sprung.

In today's Gospel, hearing of John's imprisonment, Jesus withdrew to Galilee to fulfill a prophecy of Isaiah. And with four words, "From that time on," Matthew says that Jesus inaugurated his preaching career. We are privileged to hear Jesus's one homily: "Repent, for the kingdom of heaven is at hand." He called his listeners to change their lives in light of a new dawning reality. All the other teachings of Jesus—the Beatitudes, not serving two masters, not worrying, not judging others, forgiving others, loving the enemy—indeed, the entire Sermon on the Mount that will follow in chapters 5 to 7, were simply corollaries to his insight that in his ministry, God's great dream for this world has begun to blossom. No doubt rooted in the night vision found in the Book of Daniel (7:13–14), the kingdom of heaven, through the sovereignty of God, is not only the definitive social, political, and spiritual salvation of all humanity but also the kingdom that establishes peace and justice.

To ensure that we don't think the kingdom of heaven is some airy-fairy, esoteric reality, we see that the kingdom of heaven has a down-to-earth, practical reality. Today's Gospel concludes with the sick, those afflicted with various diseases and pains, demoniacs, epileptics, and paralytics being cured by Jesus.

During this Christmas season, we continue to bask in the glow of God's love beyond all telling made manifest in the light of the kingdom of heaven.

PONDER

- If I could preach one homily, what would my message be? Why is this message important to me?
- How have I experienced the blossoming kingdom of heaven in my life?

TUESDAY AFTER EPIPHANY (OR JANUARY 8)

Food for Thought: Mark 6:34–44

Scientists tell us that there is a strong connection between food and memory. Foods that are tied to specific events such as holiday celebrations and birthdays can trigger the release of dopamine, a neurotransmitter that plays a role in how we feel pleasure. Dopamine can also create pathways in a part of the brain that can change short-term memories into long-term memories.

Fond food memories aren't just about taste, however. We remember them precisely because they activated our other four senses as well. I still remember sitting at Mary Ann's Christmas table some twenty-five years ago in Beijing. It was the beautiful table setting, the presentation of her native Indian samosas, the smell of the turkey, the taste of the wine, and the warmth of the fire that seared into my memory an unforgettable Christmas Day celebration. Clearly, food is not just about survival; it can also evoke strong memories of memorable moments.

Today's Gospel of the feeding of the five thousand is the only miracle performed by Jesus found in all four Gospels (see Matthew 14:15–21; Luke 9:12–17; John 6:1–15). A second noteworthy element is that each account has strong eucharistic overtones as Jesus takes, blesses, and breaks the loaves before giving them to the disciples to set before the people. Because food can trigger memories, one can only wonder if the experience of the Last Supper helped shape the memory of this miracle with its eucharistic overtones. Jesus's miracle might also have triggered memories of Elisha who fed one hundred men (see 2 Kings 4:42–44). Mark's portrayal of the crowd in orderly groups of fifty and a hundred suggests a level of decorum that contributes to the idea that this is a prequel to the Messianic banquet where everyone's hunger will be satiated.

Jesus's teaching about the heavenly banquet, his table fellowship with sinners, today's miracle of feeding the five thousand, and his gift of a ritual meal to be done in his memory all suggest that he knew the power of food not simply as a means of survival but also as a reminder of God's love beyond all telling made flesh in the Bread of Life.

PONDER

- What positive memories do I have associated with food?
- What does heaven as a Messianic banquet say to me?

WEDNESDAY AFTER EPIPHANY (OR JANUARY 9)

Fear Not! Mark 6:45–52

There is a common post on Instagram that states the expression "Do not be afraid" and the suggestion not to fear appear 365 times in the Bible—one for each day of the year! Lloyd John Ogilvie, Millennium in his book *Facing the Future Without Fear: Prescriptions for Courageous Living in the New Millennium* goes even further and says the biblical admonition appears 366 times—the extra one for leap year!

"It just ain't so," my Bible scholar friend, Father Bill, told me and continued, "You can't believe everything you read on the internet. A quick skim of a biblical concordance shows the idea of not fearing is found a little over one hundred times in the Old Testament and more than forty times in the New Testament."

Although the daily reminder is not biblically based, we would do well to keep it in mind every day. Within any twenty-four-hour period, we can at least once feel like the disciples in today's Gospel who are rowing against a strong wind. Our teenagers test the limits of our patience, the stock market causes us to get squeamish, a misunderstanding arises with a family member or best friend, a coworker gossips behind our back. In those situations—and more heart-wrenching ones like feeling grief over the death of a loved one, surprised by unannounced divorce papers, devastated by the loss of a home by a natural disaster—it's easy to think that Jesus is far from us.

Today's Gospel hints to the disciples being tired, frustrated, and maybe even feeling hopeless. They had been in the boat from evening on. We don't know how long they battled the strong winds, but we do know that during the fourth watch (between 3 a.m. and 4 a.m.), Jesus came walking toward them on the sea. His divinity and mastery over the laws of nature were on full display. Believing him to be a ghost, the disciples cried out in terror. It was then that Jesus challenged them, "Take courage, it is I, do not be afraid." He joined them in the boat and the wind died down.

Today's Gospel shows that God's love beyond all telling, celebrated during this season, is not simply a feel-good consolation but a personal presence that offers hope, courage, and strength when our arms are weak and the emotional winds too powerful.

PONDER

- When did I last feel as if I was rowing against strong winds? How did I react?
- In what fearful situations do I need to lean on the hope, courage, and strength that Jesus offers?

THURSDAY AFTER EPIPHANY (OR JANUARY 10)

Sent on Mission: Luke 4:14–22

Many years ago, a wise spiritual director asked a young Franciscan friar, "Why did God put you on this earth? What's your mission?" I was dumbfounded and didn't know what to say. After a few awkward moments, hoping to give the correct answer, I reverted to the answer of the old *Baltimore Catechism*: "To know, love, and serve God in this world and be happy with him forever in the next." My spiritual director chuckled. Being a spiritual director now for over forty years, I see the wisdom in having a directee know their mission.

About twenty-five years ago, I took the time to pray over and write my own mission statement. I discovered it during a weeklong retreat. "I am called to enlighten and illumine the presence of God in the wounds and worlds of the spiritual pilgrim." I do that in my preaching of parish missions and retreats as well as in my ministry as a spiritual director.

In today's Gospel, we find Jesus in the synagogue at Nazareth. Getting up to do the reading, he was handed the scroll from the prophet Isaiah. Scholars tell us the Isaiah text that Luke puts into the mouth of Jesus was not found in the synagogue scroll; rather, Luke has woven together concrete images from the Isaiah passages found in chapters 58 and 61 to avoid an over-spiritualized text. From Jesus's—and Luke's—perspective, the Spirit has called Jesus to a very practical mission: to preach good news to the poor, to open the door of prisons, to heal the blind, to free the oppressed, and to announce what would be a jubilee year of God.

Today's Gospel should challenge us to ponder our own sense of mission and the practical implications of it. Perhaps we resonate with the *Baltimore Catechism*'s call to know, love, and serve God in this world. If so, how do we do that? Hopefully, we are aware that every mission, like a coin, has two sides. One is to love and serve God, and the other is to express that in love and service of our neighbor. To emphasize the former without the latter is to live an airy-fairy spirituality that is not grounded in reality; to emphasize the latter without the former is to be a mere humanitarian and philanthropist. To do both is to walk in the light of God's love beyond all telling.

PONDER

- Why did God put me on this earth? What is my mission?
- How do I express my mission on a daily, weekly, and monthly basis?

FRIDAY AFTER EPIPHANY (OR JANUARY 11)

A Healing Touch: Luke 5:12–16

Retiring from teaching college-level biology for over forty years, Franciscan Father George volunteered at the local hospital. I was taken aback by his new ministry: rocking newborn babies twice a week. He didn't appreciate my teasing him about it.

"There's a lot more science to it than you realize, Albert. I just don't rock babies. I touch their fingers, hands, and cheeks. I make eye contact with them and softly talk to them. All this touching promotes bonding and a baby's emotional health. Touching helps regulate a baby's heart rate and breathing. It enhances the sense of security and hopefully will have an impact on the child's emotional well-being later in life. Maybe you weren't touched enough as a child and that's why you are so onery at times," Father George concluded with a devilish smile.

At the time of Jesus, people who contracted leprosy were as good as dead. They were marginalized, ostracized from the community, and considered untouchable. Lepers were unable to worship in the temple and touching them rendered a person impure. One can only imagine the despair felt by anyone who suffered from psoriasis, scabies, or syphilis, all of which were traditionally lumped in the biblical mentality under the category of leprosy.

In today's Gospel, Jesus encountered a man who no doubt was filled with desperation because he was "full of leprosy." This man's faith is on full display in his name for Jesus and in his request, "Lord, if you wish, you can make me clean."

In a stunning demonstration of compassion, Jesus stretched out his hand and touched the man, which in the eyes of observers, would have rendered the Lord impure. His touch not only healed the man of the disease but also incorporated him back into the community. It also allowed him to practice his faith again because

Jesus sent him to the priest to offer the appropriate ritual of thanksgiving.

During this Christmas season, we celebrate that God's love beyond all telling is touchable in a person of flesh and blood. We also rejoice in the compassion of Jesus who is anxious to touch and heal those areas in our lives that make us feel diseased and ostracized from family, friends, and community.

PONDER

- Who are the people that I believe are diseased and should be ostracized from the Church and the community?
- What areas in my life do I consider to be diseased and untouchable?

SATURDAY AFTER EPIPHANY (OR JANUARY 12)

A Marriage Made in Heaven: John 3:22–30

It's not often I get to meet people who have been married for forty-seven years.

"So, what's the secret?" I asked Eric and Kathy.

They must have been asked that question a million times because in unison, they simply replied, "The three C's: commitment, communication, and compromise."

Eric commented, "You have to realize that there's more to a successful marriage than simply love. Your love will be tested time and again. Are you in this relationship for the long haul even when things get testy and tough? Your love has to have stick-to-itiveness—that's what commitment is all about."

"And you have to keep talking," Kathy continued, "and never stop sharing and communicating your feelings."

"And there's got to be some give-and-take. You can never settle for the attitude that everything must be 'my way or the highway.' Compromise is critical," Eric concluded.

Based on the three C's, it's not surprising that marriage imagery has been applied to God's relationship with his people. The Old Testament's Song of Songs was viewed as an allegory that interpreted God's passionate love for his people that went far beyond a platonic relationship: Early on, the people of Israel interpreted the woman in the Song of Songs as themselves and God as their bridegroom. Christians soon adopted the idea that Christ was the bridegroom, and the soul was the bride. The twelfth-century Cistercian Bernard of Clairvaux brought this love mysticism to new heights, expanding it not only to all the books of the Bible but also to creation and one's experience. The bridal mysticism of the thirteenth century believed a profound love for God could lead to a spiritual marriage between God and the soul.

The three C's are perennial and easily apply to God's covenant with us and our relationship with God. Despite our sins and infidelities, God's love is steadfast, and he remains committed to his covenant with us. He continually communicates his enduring love, mercy, and compassion through the sacraments and in our daily experience. In today's Gospel, after comparing Christ to the bridegroom and himself to the best man who rejoices to hear the voice of the bridegroom, John reminds us of the importance of compromise as he challenges us with the words, "He must increase; I must decrease." God has a love beyond all telling for each one of us—it's a marriage made in heaven.

PONDER

- What are important personal qualities that I bring to my relationships with others and with God?
- How comfortable am I applying marriage and bridal imagery to my relationship with God? Are there other images that work better for me?

SUNDAY AFTER THE EPIPHANY OF THE LORD

BAPTISM OF THE LORD, YEAR A

A Spiritual Chiropractor: Matthew 3:13–17

I asked a few people what their baptism has meant for them. I was surprised by the variety of responses.

Kathy mentioned it took away her original sin.

"Though I don't remember it," Joe said, "it was my first experience of dying and rising with Jesus. I continue to experience that paschal dynamic in my adult life."

Joye told me it was her initiation into the Catholic faith, while thirty-year-old Sister Angela commented, "My three religious vows of poverty, chastity, and obedience are my way of bringing my baptismal promises to the next level."

Brian, a meat-and-potatoes kind of guy, put it bluntly, "It's like going to a spiritual chiropractor. It got me in alignment with God from the get-go."

Believe it or not, of all those wonderful meanings for baptism, Brian's came closest to Matthew's meaning found in today's Gospel. This version of Jesus's baptism is the only version that begins with John and Jesus discussing what is to take place. John hesitates to baptize Jesus, telling him that he should be the one to be baptized by Jesus. Jesus tells an unwilling John to baptize him "for thus it is fitting for us to fulfill all righteousness."

Sounding somewhat peculiar to twenty-first-century ears, the word "righteousness" appears seven times on the lips of Jesus in Matthew's Gospel. It's found here at the baptism. It's found five times in the Sermon on the Mount (5:6, 10, 20; 6:1, 33). In the temple, Jesus uses it to describe John the Baptist's ministry (21:32).

Righteousness suggests a right relationship with God, others, oneself, and all creation. It is the willingness to be faithful to the demands of God's covenant. It is lining up with the values of the kingdom of heaven.

Baptism is not only the removal of original sin and our immersion into the paschal mystery of Christ, but it is also, using Brian's imagery, a visit to the spiritual chiropractor who faithfully aligns our hearts with the kingdom of God's relationships.

PONDER

- What does my baptism mean to me?
- How aligned is my heart with the kingdom's values of peace, love, and justice? What values do I need to strengthen?

BAPTISM OF THE LORD, YEAR B

Spiritual Awakenings: Mark 1:7–11

See the reflection and questions for Weekdays of Christmastime: From January 2 to the Epiphany of the Lord, January 6.

BAPTISM OF THE LORD, YEAR C

A Flash of Recognition: Luke 3:15–16, 21–22

Dan's father had been estranged from his family for fifteen years. One day, while at a baseball game, Dan took a double take. *Is that Pops?* he thought. Realizing the vendor was his father, he gingerly approached him. "Excuse me," Dan said, "I don't know if you know who I am...."

The vendor stopped in his tracks. The flash of recognition was instant. Putting his right palm on Dan's chest, the vendor exclaimed with excitement, "You're my son!"

Dan struggled to hold back tears, gave his father a bear hug, and said, "Pops!"

We don't know when it first happened. As a child? As an adolescent? As a young adult? But at some moment in his life, Jesus began to have inklings of his unique relationship with God. They no doubt initially percolated up on occasion from his subconscious. Although there are passages in the Old Testament that use the metaphor of God acting like a father (for example, Deuteronomy 32:6; Psalm 103:13–14; Isaiah 63:16; Jeremiah 31:20), no one had ever had the audacity to directly address God as Father—until Jesus.

Jesus's name for God, in his native Aramaic, *Abba*, was enshrined early on in Christian literature. This informal name for a father—used both by children and adults—is found in the Second Gospel as Jesus struggles in the Garden of Gethsemane (see Mark 14:36). Paul will quote it explicitly and translate it into Greek in the Letters to the Romans (see 8:15) and the Galatians (see 4:6). The fact that "Abba" is explicitly mentioned by Mark and Paul highlights its origin with Jesus; this would have also justified it for those with sensitive or overly pious ears.

Perhaps Jesus's unique relationship with God came to full consciousness at this baptism. His Father's voice confirms his identity:

"You are my Son, the Beloved; with you I am well pleased." Perhaps it was at that very moment that Jesus himself had a flash of recognition and for the first time whispered, "Abba."

Because many of us were baptized as infants, our true identity might still remain unconscious. Hopefully, as we grow from childhood through adolescent to adulthood, we will consciously discover God as *Abba* and ourselves as beloved children of a Father who loves us with love beyond all telling.

PONDER

- When did I become consciously aware of the Father's relationship with me and who I am in his eyes?
- Besides father, what other images of God speak deeply to me and nourish my spiritual life?

Special Feasts and Memorials

DECEMBER 6: FEAST OF ST. NICHOLAS

Secret Santa

Most of us first get to know him as Santa Claus, that red-dressed, bearded man who "had a broad face and a little round belly, that shook when he laughed, like a bowl full of jelly." As children, we left him cookies and milk and hoped his journey down the chimney wouldn't be too burdensome and tight. As adults, we learn that Santa is the popularization of St. Nicholas, whose feast we celebrate today.

Legend has it that there was a poor nobleman with three daughters of marriageable age. However, this nobleman could not afford the required dowry. Fearing his daughters would consequently never get married, the man was considering sacrificing their innocence to raise the necessary funds.

Nicholas heard of the man's plight. According to one version of the legend, Nicholas climbed up on the nobleman's roof for three consecutive nights and threw gold coins down his chimney so that they would land in the girls' stockings that had been hung by the fire to dry. Hence, today's tradition arose of leaving gifts in stockings—and the belief that Santa comes down the chimney.

Nicholas was one of the first "newfangled" saints. Before St. Nicholas and the others, the only path to canonization was through martyrdom. However, with the Roman emperor's acceptance of Christianity in the fourth century and thus the end of religious persecution, new models of holiness were sought. Nicholas reminds us that holiness is no longer simply defined by spending one's life in martyrdom; it is also defined by spending one's life helping others anonymously. Every single act of charity, whether it is almsgiving, sharing time and talents, or helping the marginalized, expands the size of the heart and is noticed and blessed by God. Responding to human hungers—be they physical, emotional, psychological, or spiritual—is truly a way to give birth to God's Word with a love beyond all telling.

Ponder

- When was the last time someone anonymously helped me? What was my response?
- In what ways can I realistically stretch the size of my heart and broaden my life of charity?

DECEMBER 8: SOLEMNITY OF THE IMMACULATE CONCEPTION OF THE VIRGIN MARY

God's Dream

A father holds his newborn son, studies the infant's tiny hands, and says, "Yes, indeed, he has the hands of a Super Bowl quarterback!" A new mother marvels at the gift of her young daughter, and proudly announces, "My daughter's going to be a ballerina!" Parents have hearts brimming over with hopes, dreams, and wishes for each child as they hold in wonder the bundle of potential wrapped up in the flesh of a newborn.

Like a new parent, God had a dream for Adam and Eve and their children. God showered great potential upon them in their creation, blessed them, and made them stewards of creation. God surrounded them with peace, love, and justice, and hoped they would never experience the guilt that arises when such virtues are lacking. When they lost sight of that dream, turned toward sin, and experienced shame, God sent Jesus, divine love incarnate, to remind their descendants of the abundant possibility with which they had been created and blessed.

Today's Feast of the Immaculate Conception of the Virgin Mary is a celebration and commemoration of the deepest aspirations that God holds for humanity. Mary is the second Eve who was chosen by God "before the foundation of the world, to be holy and without blemish" (Ephesians 1:4, from the second reading) in the sight of all creation. Freed from the influence of Adam and Eve's sin from the very moment of her conception, she can accomplish everything "according to the intention of [God's] will"; indeed, she exists simply for the praise of God's glory (Ephesians 1:11–12). No wonder the archangel Gabriel greets her as one who is favored and "full of grace" (see Luke 1:28). Her life sings of the original God-intended dignity of the human condition and her unconditional "yes" to bearing the Son of God with a love beyond all telling, the realization of God's highest hopes for creation.

Just as Jesus is God's infinite love for humanity enfleshed, so Mary is God's original dream for humanity incarnate.

PONDER

- What dreams do I have for my loved ones? How can I practically help them to realize those dreams?
- What is God's dream for me? What hinders me from realizing it?

DECEMBER 12: FEAST OF OUR LADY OF GUADALUPE

The Mantle of God's Love

On December 9, 1531, at Tepeyac, a hill where the mother of the Aztec gods had been worshipped, fifty-seven-year-old Juan Diego, responding to a voice calling him by name, met a young mestiza, a woman of Native American and European heritage. She wore a red tunic, symbol of royalty among the Aztecs, and a blue cloak, symbol of the gods. She was arrayed as a goddess queen with the radiance of the sun behind her. Her hands were folded in the Aztec symbol of service and submission. With what could only be described as a twenty-first-century missionary sensitivity, she confirmed her posture with the widower, whose native land had recently been conquered by Spanish-speaking foreigners, by speaking to him in his native Nahuatl, saying, "Listen and let it penetrate your heart...do not be troubled or weighed down with grief. Do not fear any illness or vexation, anxiety, or pain. Am I not here who am your Mother? Are you not under my shadow and protection?...Are you not in the folds of my mantle? In the crossing of my arms? Is there anything else you need?"

La Morenita—"the little brown one"—wore a black cord beneath her breasts, the knot visible below her hands. This was the Aztec symbol of pregnancy—and the flower on her womb the symbol of the new life and the new era her Son would bring to the land of the Americas.

Mary's pregnancy and today's feast remind us that Christ was not only to be born in the Middle East but in every land and every culture. Indeed, the mantle of God's love beyond all telling covers the entire earth.

What the Spanish Franciscan friars previously had struggled to do with little success, Our Lady of Guadalupe accomplished in just nine years—the conversion and baptism of over eight million native Mexicans. She truly is the patroness of the Americas.

PONDER

- How do I see my culture as blessed by God? In what areas does my culture need conversion?
- What role does Mary play in my daily life? What gifts can God offer me through Mary's intercession?

DECEMBER 13: FEAST OF ST. LUCY

A Light in the Darkness

Along with Agatha of Sicily, Agnes of Rome, Cecilia of Rome, and Catherine of Alexandria, today's saint, Lucy, is one of the best-known virgin martyrs. She is one of the few women mentioned in the first Eucharistic Prayer in the celebration of Mass. A Caribbean country and several places in the Philippines are named after her. A popular song, often sung by the gondoliers of Venice, has her name in its title.

Lucy's name comes from the Latin word for light, *lux*. Several traditions, especially in Scandinavian countries where people eat saffron buns and gingerbread cookies on this day, incorporate a symbolic meaning of St. Lucy as the bearer of light in the darkness of winter. Before calendar reforms, her feast once coincided with the winter solstice, the shortest day of the year. Consequently, it became a festival of light.

Like many early martyrs, we know very little about the life of fourth-century Lucy. A late fifteenth-century tradition states she was tortured by eye-gouging. Another version has Lucy taking her own eyes out to discourage a persistent suitor who admired them. This is one of the reasons why she is patron saint of people with eye illnesses. Although traditions about her abound, what we know as historical fact is simply this: a disappointed suitor accused Lucy of being a Christian, and she was executed in Syracuse, Sicily, in the year 304 during the persecution of the Christians by Diocletian.

In these dark days of winter that often mirror world events, St. Lucy, true to her name, offers us some light about Christian living. As a martyr (the Greek word *martyria* literally means "witness"), she testified with the witness of her daily life to the truth of Christ and challenges us to do the same. But she doesn't stop there. This disciple made herself like her master and conformed herself to

Christ by the shedding of her blood. As St. Augustine noted, martyrs love Christ in this life and imitate him in death. To give one's very life for the sake of Christ is the most precious gift and supreme proof of one's love beyond all telling.

PONDER

- In what practical ways am I a martyr, a witness, to Christ in my daily life?
- Among my family and friends, who are the bearers of light?

DECEMBER 14: FEAST OF ST. JOHN OF THE CROSS

The Dark Side of Grace

God's grace is a gift that often comes out of nowhere. We sometimes experience it as a presence when we pray, as a listening ear and a shoulder to cry on when we grieve the loss of a loved one, as the love of a friend, spouse, or a child, as the strength and courage to make a difficult decision that will change our lives. It manifests itself as mercy, forgiveness, and compassion. Grace is the divine ray of sunshine that peeks through the thick, dark clouds of life.

But there is another side to grace, a dark side. That's the insight that today's saint, the great Carmelite mystic of the sixteenth century John of the Cross, offers us.

Although he never used the expression the "dark night of the soul," John of the Cross did refer to two nights. Each is a unique divine grace given to us as we mature in the life of prayer.

A person who commits to daily prayer quickly begins to experience feelings of peace, joy, and contentment. These feelings entice the person to keep returning to the daily time of prayer. Soon, the person judges "a successful period of prayer" with these feelings. Occasionally, a person makes the mistake of equating these gifts with the Giver himself, God.

The "night of the senses," occurring about six months into the commitment to prayer, is a natural consequence of daily prayer. The feelings of peace, joy, and contentment are taken away and dissipate. Although we might fear we are doing something wrong or have offended God, this is actually a grace from God that purifies our intentions for praying. We pray not for what we get out of it but simply to be with God.

The "night of the spirit" is a more intense experience of grace that challenges our spiritual smugness. Just when we think we are making spiritual progress and consider ourselves "right with God," this grace raises doubts about our fidelity to God's will. We feel our years of praying have only led us to a slippery slope where we teeter on falling into sin and failing. Our image of God is not only challenged but destroyed as the God we believed in disappears. This occurs so that the *presence* of God, and not simply our *mental image* or picture of God, can come more deeply into our lives. This second purifying night is also truly a grace because it reminds us that God is an utter mystery before whom we can only humbly bow.

John of the Cross reminds us that we sometimes experience the purifying action of grace as darkness.

PONDER

- How did I respond when the feelings of peace, joy, and contentment in daily prayer were taken away from me?
- How did I respond when my mental image of God was proven to be inadequate or faulty or threatened?

JANUARY 2: MEMORIAL OF ST. BASIL THE GREAT AND ST. GREGORY NAZIANZEN, BISHOPS AND DOCTORS OF THE CHURCH

Defenders of the Faith

Many Christians are not aware of the fact that early Christianity was a work in progress. It would take more than three hundred years for Christianity not only to define its doctrines but also to correctly understand the interpretation of those doctrines. Perhaps the most difficult doctrine to interpret was the Trinity, the belief that there was one God existing in three coeternal, consubstantial divine persons: God the Father, God the Son (Jesus Christ), and God the Holy Spirit, three distinct persons sharing one nature.

In the fourth century, Arianism was popular. It taught that the Father existed prior to the Son who was not, by nature, God but rather a changeable creature who was granted the dignity of becoming "Son of God." It was popular in both the Eastern and Western Roman empires, even after the Council of Nicaea in 325 condemned it as a heresy.

The clear teaching and brave episcopal leadership of St. Basil the Great and St. Gregory Nazianzen helped to put an end to the Arian heresy, but not without personal hardship and tribulation. They suffered physical attacks and threats from the emperor, many bishops, and other clergy and laity, and yet, through it all, they remained fierce defenders of the orthodox interpretation of the Trinity.

What is often overlooked is that these two defenders of the faith nurtured a deep and vibrant prayer life. Both men spent years in solitude and prayer as hermits at different stages of their lives. Basil even wrote a collection of his responses to questions about the ascetic life, which became the foundation for the rule of life for the monastery he founded in 356. It was no doubt their prayer life that gave Basil and Gregory the strength, tenacity, and conviction to stand up to the heretical Arians.

As we honor Basil and Gregory today, we are reminded that our prayer life is not done in a hermetically sealed jar; rather, it must influence how we live. Indeed, what happens *after* our prayer time is more important than what happens *during* our prayer time.

PONDER

- How does my prayer time challenge me to defend the faith among my family, friends, and coworkers?
- How do I experience the Trinity in my daily prayer?

JANUARY 3: THE MOST HOLY NAME OF JESUS

What's in a Name?

I was named Albert after my grandfather. Within hours after my baptism, however, an elderly Ursuline nun pronounced my name in her native French, "Al-bear"—with no *T* pronounced. It was a smash hit! "So unique, so different, so sophisticated. Maybe he'll go places if we use that pronunciation," the shoe salesman of Russian descent and his wife thought. So my parents decided to adopt the French pronunciation. As I grew up, it became a source of confusion for others. When I introduce myself, many people initially respond, "Nice to meet you, Father Bear." I have to correct them and say, "No, it's like Teddy Bear—but it's Albert." My parents didn't realize that an air of sophistication has its disadvantages.

Today's celebration reminds us of the sanctity of the name of Jesus. His name effects what it means. In first-century Judaism, the name Jesus in Hebrew, *Jeshua*, literally meant "Yahweh helps." This was often interpreted as "Yahweh saves." Thus, the angel tells Joseph that Mary "will bear a son, and you are to name him Jesus, for he will save his people from their sins" (Matthew 1:21). In today's Gospel about the child's circumcision, Joseph and Mary name their baby "Jesus."

The early Church recognized the power of Jesus's name. To the crippled man at the Beautiful Gate, Peter said, "I have no silver or gold, but what I have I give you; in the name of Jesus Christ of Nazareth, stand up and walk" (Acts 3:6). Peter later proclaimed to the Sanhedrin that it was by the name of Jesus Christ that the crippled man was able to walk (see Acts 4:10–12). He concluded with a statement that astonished his listeners: "There is salvation in no one else, for there is no other name under heaven given among mortals by which we must be saved."

In what scholars believe to be an early baptismal hymn found at the end of today's first reading, the name of Jesus is proclaimed to be "above every name," and at its proclamation "every knee should bend in heaven and on earth and under the earth."

"What's in a name?" is a famous line from William Shakespeare's play *Romeo and Juliet*. Juliet rhetorically asks this to express the idea that a person's name is not important, but one's true identity is what matters. The Christian tradition takes issue with Juliet's implication because Jesus's identity, mission, and power as Savior are inextricably bound to his name.

PONDER

- How do I react when I hear someone take the name of Jesus in vain?
- How would using the name of Jesus in my prayer strengthen my spiritual life?

JANUARY 4: ST. ELIZABETH ANN SETON

The Secret to Holiness

Two years before the signing of the Declaration of Independence, Elizabeth Ann Bayley was born in New York City to a high society couple. She was raised in what became, in the years after the American Revolution, the Episcopal Church. At the age of nineteen, she married the wealthy twenty-five-year-old William Magee Seton. Socially prominent in New York City, the Setons lived in a residence on Wall Street. Along with her dearest friend, she continued the social ministry she had learned from her stepmother and nursed the sick and dying among her family, friends, and needy neighbors. After nine years of marriage, Elizabeth's husband died of tuberculosis and left the widow with five daughters to raise. She was received into the Catholic Church in 1805. To support herself and her children, she opened an academy for young ladies, a venture not uncommon for widows of social standing at the time. In 1809, at the invitation of the Sulpician priests, she moved to Maryland and opened a school dedicated to the education of Catholic girls, marking the start of the Catholic parochial school system. In that same year she founded a religious community dedicated to the care of children of the poor. She spent her final years leading her new congregation. She died in 1821 at the age of forty-six. Pope Paul VI canonized her on September 14, 1975.

What was the secret to holiness for this accomplished wife, mother, and founder of a religious community whose life had numerous twists and turns? A prayer she herself wrote reveals the secret: "Oh, Father, the first rule of our dear Savior's life was to do Your Will. Let His Will of the present moment be the first rule of our daily life and work, with no other desire but for its most full and complete accomplishment. Help us to follow it faithfully, so that doing what You wish, we will be pleasing to You. Amen."

St. Elizabeth Ann Seton's prayer reminds us that we are called to imitate Jesus by doing the will of the Father. That will is made evident in the task of the present moment. By responding to the unmet need or required duty of what is before us (it might be caring for a sick spouse, raising children, or attending to the needs of the unfortunate, all tasks done by today's saint), God's love beyond all telling is poured out into the lives of others. In doing that will of God, we grow in holiness.

PONDER

- What is God asking of me in this present moment? How am I responding?
- What do I find inspiring about the life of St. Elizabeth Ann Seton?